stoCKPIling
STRATEGIC
MATERIALS

sTOCKPILING
STRATEGIC
MATERIALS

An Evaluation of the National Program

Raymond F. Mikesell

American Enterprise Institute for Public Policy Research
Washington, D.C.

Raymond F. Mikesell is professor of economics at the University of Oregon and during 1981–1984 was a member of the National Materials Advisory Board.

Library of Congress Cataloging-in-Publication Data

Mikesell, Raymond Frech.
  Stockpiling strategic materials.

  (AEI studies ; 431)
  1. Strategic materials—Government policy—United States. 2. Mineral industries—Government policy—United States. 3. United States—National security.
I. Title. II. Series.
HC110.S8M54 1986   333.8'511'0973   86-3612
ISBN 0-8447-3588-4 (alk. paper)

1 3 5 7 9 10 8 6 4 2

AEI Studies 431

Printed in the United States of America

Contents

Foreword

U.S. concern about vulnerability to the disruption of imports of strategic and critical minerals dates from the 1930s, and the basic stockpile legislation was enacted in 1946. The National Defense Stockpile program has been subject over the years to a variety of criticisms, both inside and outside the government. It has been reviewed by national commissions and in special reports, many prepared by government agencies.

The program does not protect the U.S. civilian economy from supply disruptions caused by cartels, embargoes, limited wars, or civil disturbances in foreign areas producing strategic or critical materials on which the United States depends. A number of studies have therefore been made of the vulnerability of the economy to disruptions of foreign supplies of nonfuel minerals in peacetime and of proposals for government action to avoid or mitigate the economic effects of such disruptions. But no comprehensive, analytical study has encompassed all the issues relating to U.S. vulnerability to disruption of imports of critical minerals.

In this study Professor Raymond Mikesell integrates and evaluates the existing literature as a basis for determining national policy. Mikesell, who has conducted research in natural resources for nearly forty years and has served as a consultant on mineral problems and strategic materials to a number of companies and U.S. government agencies, reviews the history of the National Defense Stockpile program and evaluates the criticisms that have been made of it, together with proposals for legislative and administrative changes. He also examines the vulnerability of the civilian economy to disruptions of imports in peacetime and evaluates various proposals for dealing with this vulnerability. He concludes with recommendations for reforming the National Defense Stockpile program and for addressing the civilian economy's peacetime vulnerability.

WILLIAM J. BAROODY, JR.
President
American Enterprise Institute

vii

Preface

This study is based on my research on stockpiling supported by the joint Mineral Economics and Policy Program of Pennsylvania State University and Resources for the Future, directed by Hans H. Landsberg, senior fellow, Resources for the Future, and John E. Tilton, professor of mineral economics, Pennsylvania State University. The National Defense Stockpile (NDS) has been the subject of many books and articles and thousands of pages of congressional hearings and government reports over the past half-century. In view of President Reagan's proposal of July 1985 calling for a drastic reduction in the NDS goals, a review and an appraisal of the program seem timely. In addition to providing a short history and critique of the program, I have examined several proposals for amending or supplementing it that have been put forward in recent years.

Although I am solely responsible for the interpretations and judgments made in this study, I want to express my appreciation to Lincoln Anderson, Shirley Kessel, F. Taylor Ostrander, Simon D. Strauss, and John E. Tilton for their comments on a preliminary draft of the manuscript.

1
Introduction

The National Defense Stockpile (NDS) has had a long and stormy history since the 1930s. The program grew from U.S. experience in two world wars, and the present program was formulated to deal with anticipated shortages of strategic materials in a future war closely resembling World War II. It is not surprising, therefore, that critics of the program have objected to the focus on conventional war as being highly improbable and having a low priority in an age of intercontinental nuclear weapons. Yet critics have not devised alternatives for the function of a strategic stockpile. One purpose of this study is to suggest other approaches to the objectives and design of the program.

From the beginning the NDS program has been beset by conflict between two methods of protecting the defense program and its supporting industrial base from shortages of strategic materials during a major war. One method is to accumulate a stockpile sufficient to cover shortfalls of supplies below projected requirements; the other is to expand domestic output to reduce or eliminate the shortfalls. The latter approach was embodied in Title III of the Defense Production Act of 1950, but activities under the act have involved the NDS since purchases of domestic output under authority of the act were eventually added to NDS inventories. This approach also involved the NDS more directly when stockpile objectives were manipulated to provide a market for the output of the domestic mining industry. Strong congressional criticism ensued of the use of the NDS to support the interests of the mining industry, a criticism with which President John F. Kennedy expressed considerable sympathy.

During the Nixon administration the conventional-war premise of the NDS was rejected, and President Richard M. Nixon proposed that 90 percent of the existing inventory be liquidated. Nixon's action was criticized as an attempt to use the stockpile for budgetary and anti-inflationary purposes, but his rejection of the basic premise was not seriously debated. That premise was restored during the Ford and Carter administrations, when stockpile goals were based on preparation for a possible nonnuclear war in Europe.

Another question that has arisen is whether the stockpile should be used solely for defense or for both defense and civilian production. If the latter, how should stockpile materials be allocated for civilian use? The original stockpile objectives were mainly limited to defense uses, but as the conventional war concept evolved, the objectives were estimated both for meeting defense requirements and for maintaining essential civilian production in wartime. Some congressmen and administration spokesmen argued for the use of the stockpile to support all civilian production except luxury items, while others advocated a stockpile oriented to defense and essential civilian requirements. A related conflict has to do with the availability of stockpile materials for shortages in periods other than a major war. Although it has generally been agreed that the stockpile should be available to support defense production in peacetime, some have advocated that it be available for civilian production or that a separate economic stockpile be established to meet civilian requirements in peacetime.

The present NDS program is based on a war mobilization plan that provides for stockpile inventories sufficient to support defense and civilian production in a wartime economy subject to moderate austerity. In part the conflicts over the use of the stockpile arise from an ambiguity in the concept of national defense, which can be defined narrowly in terms of military requirements or more broadly in terms of a civilian economy capable of providing maximum support for the defense effort.

What Are Strategic Materials?

There is no standard definition of a strategic material, but most definitions state that the material is necessary for producing military and essential civilian goods and services and that requirements may exceed domestic and foreign supplies in the event of supply disruptions.[1] Whether any particular material is regarded as strategic depends on a judgment about whether and how much of the material is essential in production, how essential the products are for which the material is required, and the probability of contingencies that would lead to disruption of normal supplies. In March 1984 NDS goals had been established for fifty-eight materials or commodity groups (see table 1). Some material specialists would exclude metals such as copper and nickel, and a number of congressmen are demanding the reinstatement of silver. Much depends on the probabil-

TABLE 1
NATIONAL DEFENSE STOCKPILE INVENTORY OF STRATEGIC AND CRITICAL MATERIALS, MARCH 31, 1984

Commodity	Unit	Goal	Inventory
Aluminum metal group	ST Al metal	7,150,000	4,043,784
Aluminum oxide, abrasive grain group	ST ab grain	638,000	259,124
Antimony	ST	36,000	38,841
Asbestos, amosite	ST	17,000	38,495
Asbestos, chrysotile	ST	3,000	10,751
Bauxite, refractory	LCT	1,400,000	199,926
Beryllium metal group	ST Be metal	1,220	1,061
Bismuth	LB	2,200,000	2,081,298
Cadmium	LB	11,700,000	6,328,809
Chromite, refractory grade ore	SDT	850,000	391,414
Chromium, chemical and metallurgical group	ST Cr metal	1,353,000	1,315,823
Cobalt	LB Co	85,400,000	46,193,915
Columbium group	LB Cb metal	4,850,000	2,532,419
Copper	ST	1,000,000	29,048
Cordage fibers, abaca	LB	155,000,000	0
Cordage fibers, sisal	LB	60,000,000	0
Diamond, industrial group	KT	29,700,000	37,048,492
Fluorspar, acid grade	SDT	1,400,000	895,983
Fluorspar, metallurgical grade	SDT	1,700,000	411,738
Graphite, natural, Ceylon, amorphous lump	ST	6,300	5,498
Graphite, natural, Malagasy, crystalline	ST	20,000	17,880
Graphite, natural, other sources	ST	2,800	2,804
Iodine	LB	5,800,000	7,450,930
Jewel bearings	PC	120,000,000	71,951,970
Lead	ST	1,100,000	601,025
Manganese, chemical and metallurgical group	ST Mn metal	1,500,000	1,954,922
Manganese, dioxide, battery grade group	SDT	87,000	215,505
Mercury	FL	10,500	176,515
Mica muscovite block, stained and better	LB	6,200,000	5,212,445
Mica muscovite film, 1st and 2nd qualities	LB	90,000	1,179,537

(Table continues)

TABLE 1 (continued)

Commodity	Unit	Goal	Inventory
Mica muscovite splittings	LB	12,630,000	17,388,788
Mica phlogopite block	LB	210,000	130,745
Mica phlogopite splittings	LB	930,000	1,641,699
Molybdenum group	LB Mo	0	0
Morphine sulphate and related analgesics	AMA Lb	130,000	71,303
Natural insulation fibers	LB	1,500,000	0
Nickel	ST Ni + Co	200,000	32,209
Platinum group metals, iridium	Tr Oz	98,000	26,590
Platinum group metals, palladium	Tr Oz	3,000,000	1,255,008
Platinum group metals, platinum	Tr Oz	1,310,000	452,642
Pyrethrum	LB	500,000	0
Quartz crystals	LB	600,000	2,063,936
Quinidine	Av Oz	10,100,000	1,874,504
Quinine	Av Oz	4,500,000	3,246,164
Ricinoleic/sebacic acid products	LB	22,000,000	12,524,242
Rubber	MT	864,000	120,882
Rutile	SDT	106,000	39,186
Sapphire and ruby	KT	0	16,305,502
Silicon carbide, crude	ST	29,000	80,550
Silver, fine	Tr Oz	0	137,505,946
Talc, steatite block and lump	ST	28	1,081
Tantalum group	LB Ta metal	7,160,000	2,426,387
Thorium nitrate	LB	600,000	7,131,812
Tin	MT	42,700	190,354
Titanium sponge	ST	195,000	32,331
Tungsten group	LB W metal	50,666,000	77,472,074
Vanadium group	ST V metal	8,700	541
Vegetable tannin extract, chestnut	LT	5,000	14,082
Vegetable tannin extract, quebracho	LT	28,000	131,250
Vegetable tannin extract, wattle	LT	15,000	15,001
Zinc	ST	1,425,000	378,316

NOTE: Abbreviations for unit: AMA Lb = anhydrous morphine alkaloid (pounds); AV Oz = avoirdupois ounces; FL = flask (76-pound); KT = carat; LB = pounds; LB Cb = pounds of contained columbium; LB Co = pounds of contained cobalt; LB Mo = pounds of contained molybdenum; LB Ta = pounds of contained tantalum; LB

ities assigned to contingencies that would lead to disruptions of foreign supplies. Iron ore is quite essential, for example, but the United States and Canada together are self-sufficient in it. If a very low probability were assigned to a major conventional war, only materials largely supplied from a small number of sources in developing countries would be included in the list of strategic materials. Stockpile goals for the NDS, however, are established precisely for a planned economy during a conventional war.

All but nine of the fifty-eight strategic materials for which NDS goals have been established are minerals, and the goals for other materials constitute a very small portion of the total value. Most of the materials are those for which the United States depends heavily on imports from countries other than Canada, but there are important exceptions, such as copper and lead.[2] Most materials in the stockpile are ores or other unprocessed materials, but some are refined metals, such as aluminum, cobalt, ferrochromium, and ferromanganese, because of a shortage of domestic processing capacity.[3]

A recent publication by the Office of Technology Assessment (OTA) listed thirteen strategic minerals that are essential to the national economy and for which the United States depends substantially or entirely on foreign sources that are relatively vulnerable to disruption.[4] The OTA study places four of these minerals—chromium, cobalt, manganese, and platinum-group metals—in the first tier of strategic materials and the remaining nine in the second tier. In preparing this list it was assumed that no major war during which foreign sources and transportation would be unavailable in large areas of the world would occur. The strategic materials and priorities were selected on the basis of essentiality and vulnerability to supply disruption in peacetime. Some investigators would add bauxite-alumina to the first tier; some would exclude tin from the list because substitutes exist for most of its applications. Although with few exceptions satisfactory substitutes exist for most strategic materials, often at a considerable increase in cost, substitution of more abundant materials requires considerable time, so that stockpiling may be necessary to allow adjustment of production.

Since World War II relatively few major disruptions of imported supplies of strategic materials have occurred. In 1949 the Soviet Union stopped exporting manganese and chromium ore to the

W = pounds of contained tungsten; LCT = long calcined tons; LDT = long dry tons; LT = long tons; MT = metric tons; PC = pieces; SDT = short dry tons; ST = short tons; ST Ni + Co = short tons of contained nickel plus cobalt; ST V = short tons of contained vanadium; Tr Oz = troy ounces.

SOURCE: Federal Emergency Management Agency, *Stockpile Report to the Congress, October 1983–March 1984* (Washington, D.C., October 1984), table 2, p. 22.

United States, but supplies were soon replaced by exports from South Africa. A second interruption occurred during the 1966 United Nations embargo on purchases of Rhodesian chromite, but the embargo was not effective and was offset by supplies from other sources. In 1969 a nickel industry strike in Canada occurring at a time of strong demand for nickel caused a sharp rise in prices for a few months. Finally, the 1978–1979 invasion of Shaba Province in Zaire impaired the production of cobalt and set off a wave of panic buying that raised open-market cobalt prices several-fold for a short time. No actual reduction occurred, however, in shipments of cobalt from the two largest producers, Zaire and Zambia. In all these cases the principal result was a rise in price, and there was no evidence that essential military or civilian production was impaired.

The Arab oil embargo and the action of the OPEC cartel in raising petroleum prices several-fold during the 1970s raised fears that embargoes or cartels might be instituted for several strategic materials, including bauxite, but most observers now see little possibility that this will occur in the foreseeable future.[5] Nevertheless, regional wars or civil disturbances in countries supplying a substantial portion of U.S. imports of strategic materials are believed to be relatively likely over the next decade or so. Therefore, a strategic stockpile could play an important role in offsetting disruptions of foreign supply. Under present legislation, however, materials from the NDS may be released in peacetime only for defense use.

Issues Addressed in This Study

The principal purpose of this study is to identify and analyze the major policy issues related to the NDS program. The most important issue concerns the nature of the national emergencies that the NDS should be designed to serve. This issue has been raised a number of times over the past forty years, a time during which the predicated national emergencies have several times been changed. The basic function of the NDS—to ensure sufficient strategic materials to meet requirements during a three-year conventional war—has been endorsed by Presidents Ronald Reagan, Jimmy Carter, and Gerald Ford, but that does not mean that the issue has been satisfactorily resolved. In 1983 President Reagan directed the National Security Council (NSC) to undertake a major review of the NDS program, including stockpile goals. In July 1985 a White House press release stated that on the basis of the NSC report (which had not been released at the time of writing), President Reagan proposed a cut in current stockpile requirements from $16.3 billion to $6.7 billion, of which $6.0 billion would constitute a "supplementary reserve." Clearly such a drastic cut implies a fundamental alteration in the function of the stockpile.

A second issue has to do with the criteria for determining stockpile goals. These criteria deal with such questions as the amount and composition of civilian consumption that should be supported by stockpile releases in periods of national emergency. A substantial portion of the current goals, for example, perhaps two-thirds, would be needed to maintain civilian consumption during a three-year conventional war.

A third issue is the availability of the stockpile to meet nondefense requirements in the event of disruptions of the supply of strategic materials in periods other than a major war.

A fourth issue is the relation between stockpiling and subsidizing domestic production of materials as a means of ensuring their availability in times of national emergency. This issue has been debated throughout the history of the NDS program and is of major importance today.

Finally, a number of issues have to do with the acquisition of materials and the disposal of inventories in excess of goals. These include the use of barter to acquire strategic materials in exchange for surplus agricultural commodities.

Criticisms of the NDS program have given rise to a number of proposals to change or supplement it. There is strong support within the government for subsidizing domestic production of strategic materials to reduce the size of the NDS goals or provide domestic sources for stockpile inventories. There are proposals to expand the objectives of the NDS to include protecting civilian production against disruptions of the import of strategic materials in peacetime or to establish a separate economic stockpile or a government program to expand private inventories of strategic materials. Finally, there are proposals to change the method of calculating the stockpile goals. These proposals are evaluated in chapter 5. In chapter 6 I put forward my own suggestions for revising the present NDS program.

Notes

1. U.S. stockpile legislation refers to "strategic and critical materials," "critical" referring to essentiality or the adverse effect on the civilian economy and defense industries that would occur if supplies were disrupted. The use of both terms seems redundant, since essentiality and the possibility of supply disruption are included in the term "strategic." For a good discussion see U.S. Office of Technology Assessment, *Strategic Materials: Technologies to Reduce U.S. Import Vulnerability—Summary* (Washington, D.C., 1985), pp. 11–14.

2. It is reported that Mexico is no longer considered a secure source of strategic materials.

3. Aluminum is stockpiled not because of a shortage of U.S. capacity for producing aluminum from alumina but because the United States depends substantially on foreign sources of alumina as well as bauxite.

4. The minerals are bauxite, beryllium, chromium, cobalt, columbium, diamonds (industrial), graphite, manganese, platinum-group metals, rutile, tantalum, tin, and vanadium. Office of Technology Assessment, *Strategic Materials*, p. 15.

5. For a discussion of the vulnerability to disruptions of foreign supplies in peacetime, see Raymond F. Mikesell, "Economic Stockpiles for Dealing with Vulnerability to Disruption of Foreign Supplies of Minerals," *Materials and Society*, vol. 9, no. 1 (1985), pp. 76–79.

2
Legislative and Administrative History of the National Defense Stockpile Program

The legislative and administrative history of the NDS program is long and complex, covering more than fifty years and embodying dozens of congressional bills and laws and thousands of pages of testimony and administrative reports.[1] Only the highlights are covered in this study, which emphasizes public policies and the underlying views and motives of legislators and administrators concerned with the NDS program.

Governmental interest in stockpiling of strategic materials dates from the early 1920s. The United States was short of a number of materials at the time of its entry into both World Wars I and II. These materials included metals, such as bauxite, manganese, and tin, and nonminerals, such as industrial fibers, quinine, and natural rubber, for which this country depended mainly on foreign sources. The United States was also short of some materials, such as copper, in which it was normally self-sufficient. Despite the fact that the United States had two or more years' warning before both world wars that it might become involved, virtually no government stockpile existed before World War I and only small inventories of a few materials before World War II.

Although several attempts were made to secure a general stockpiling enabling act in the 1930s, the first comprehensive stockpile legislation was the Strategic and Critical Materials Stock Piling Act of 1939 (Public Law 117).[2] Owing to heavy materials requirements during World War II, little stockpile accumulation occurred under this act. Nevertheless, many of the provisions and concepts embodied in the 1939 act, together with the issues debated before its passage, carried over to the Strategic and Critical Materials Stock Piling Act of 1946, under which (with amendments) the NDS program is now operating.

Although the orientation of the 1939 stockpiling act was primarily toward providing materials required during a war emergency, other sectoral economic and national policy interests were reflected in the legislation. In addition to providing for the acquisition of stocks of strategic materials, the 1939 act stated that it was the policy of Congress "to encourage the further development of mines and deposits of these materials in the United States, and to decrease and prevent wherever possible a dangerous and costly dependence of the United States upon foreign nations for supplies of these materials in times of national emergency." In support of this policy the act required that purchases for the stockpile be, as far as practicable, from domestic supplies of materials in excess of current industrial demand and in accordance with the Buy American Act of 1933. Agencies of the U.S. government were also directed to investigate the possibility of developing low-grade domestic deposits of minerals essential to defense or industrial needs. Another nondefense interest was served by a companion act of August 11, 1939 (Public Law 387), which provided for the exchange of surplus agricultural commodities held by the Commodity Credit Corporation (CCC) for stocks of strategic materials produced abroad. The interest of the U.S. mining industry and its representatives in Congress in using the NDS program to promote domestic mining and the interest in using the NDS program to dispose of surplus agricultural commodities have continued to be important in the evolution of the strategic stockpile program.

Negotiations to establish a post–World War II stockpile program were carried on in both the executive and the legislative branches of the government through much of the war. The War and Navy departments wanted a stockpile that would serve only national defense, with stockpile releases limited to a period of wartime emergency and acquisitions determined solely by national defense requirements. The military agencies also wanted full policy control.

The Department of the Interior wanted the stockpile program to be used to develop domestic minerals. The Department of Commerce favored flexibility in disposing of stockpile inventories to combat high prices in peacetime and wanted both acquisition and disposal to take into account the welfare of the civilian economy. The Department of State and the Federal Economic Administration also favored flexibility in both disposal and acquisition to implement U.S. foreign economic policy, such as foreign economic development. The Department of State opposed any preference for domestic materials, in part because preferences contradicted U.S. free-trade policy and in part because it wanted to avoid an abrupt decline in U.S. purchases of raw materials from foreign countries.

The final decision among three rival departmental bills was made by President Harry Truman. The approved administration bill sent to the Senate Committee on Military Affairs in 1945 reflected a compromise of the various positions within the executive branch. Policy control of the stockpile program under this bill was located in the Office of War Mobilization and Reconversion (OWMR) in the Executive Office of the President rather than in military agencies. The position of the military that stockpile releases be made only in a wartime emergency won the day over the flexible disposal position of the Departments of Commerce and State. The policy on using acquisitions to promote domestic production of minerals was left somewhat ambiguous.[3]

The debate in the executive branch over the nature and control of the postwar stockpile program was precipitated by a bill introduced in 1943 by Senator James Scrugham of Nevada.[4] The bill was aimed at maintaining the high-cost domestic mines that operated during the war with the assistance of premium prices and subsidies. It provided that stockpile purchases be made at prices high enough to keep those mines profitable and that no foreign materials be purchased for the stockpile if they were available from domestic sources. The bill was opposed by all executive agencies except the Interior Department and was not acted on by Congress. In 1945 a bill drafted by the American Mining Congress was introduced by Senator Elbert Thomas of Utah and Representative Andrew May of Kentucky. The Thomas-May bill made stockpile purchases subject to the Buy American Act of 1933 and placed administrative supervision of stockpiling under the Army-Navy Munitions Board (ANMB) but subjected sales from the stockpile and stockpile goals to close congressional supervision.

Certain features of the Thomas-May bill, including the Buy American Act provision, were combined with the approved administration bill in the Senate Committee on Military Affairs, and the compromise bill was passed by the Senate on December 20, 1945. After further changes in the bill by the House Committee on Military Affairs and approval by both houses of Congress, the stockpiling act of 1946 was signed by President Truman on July 23, 1946.

The Strategic and Critical Materials Stock Piling Act of 1946

The Strategic and Critical Materials Stock Piling Act of 1946 (Public Law 520) was passed as an amendment to the 1939 stockpiling act, and the two basic purposes of the 1939 act—to provide for the acquisition of materials for use in a wartime emergency and to encourage the development of materials in the United States to reduce dependence on foreign nations—were retained in the 1946 act. These two purposes led to a serious conflict, which was never fully resolved in the implementation of the act. The issue was further complicated by the Defense Production Act of 1950, which for a time resulted in the accumulation of two stockpiles. The complex interagency structure set up to administer the 1946 act and the sharp policy differences among the agencies caused uncertainty about the purpose of the act and impaired its implementation.[5]

The 1946 act authorized the secretaries of war, navy, and the interior, acting jointly through the ANMB, to determine which materials were to be stockpiled. Differences among the Interior Department and the two defense agencies and among members of the Strategic Materials Committee (which included the Departments of State, Treasury, Interior, Agriculture, and Commerce) reflected varying economic objectives. The act appeared to settle the question whether the stockpile should be used to stabilize prices since it stated that releases should be made "only (a) on order of the President at any time when in his judgment such release is required for purposes of common defense, or (b) in time of war or during a national emergency with respect to common defense proclaimed by the President." It did not, however, prevent purchases for the stockpile for price stabilization or other nondefense purposes.[6] Moreover, inventories in the stockpile in excess of goals were from time to time sold to stabilize prices.

One of the issues debated after the 1946 act was passed was the size of the stockpile inventory. The strategic assumptions for estimating shortfalls in supplies in the event of a global war, made by the Joint Chiefs of Staff (JCS), were that the Western Hemisphere and much of East Asia and Africa would be accessible in wartime.[7] These assumptions greatly limited the required size of the stockpile, in contrast to an assumption that supplies in wartime would be available only from Canada. The Interior Department's representative on the Strategic Materials Committee, Elmer Pehrson, argued that the JCS underestimated U.S. vulnerability to supply disruption in a general war, that no supplies could be counted on from areas outside the Western Hemisphere, and that even those supplies should be heavily discounted to take account of shipping losses and adverse political developments.[8] Pehrson had some impressive economic and strategic arguments for a larger stockpile, but a larger stockpile also corresponded with the Interior Department's interest in stimulating domestic mining. Pehrson also argued that the ANMB's estimates of civilian requirements were too low and that stockpile goals should be raised to permit higher civilian production.

In rebutting the arguments of the Interior representative, the ANMB, in addition to defending the competence of the JCS to make strategic estimates, made an interesting point that I refer to later in my critical evaluation of the NDS program. It was simply that the selection of all defense programs within the budgetary limits established by Congress involved taking a "calculated risk" and that there was no justification for taking fewer calculated risks in stockpiling than in other defense programs.[9] Security would not be maximized by spending for strategic materials money that would yield more security if invested in tanks or airplanes. The ANMB position also suggested by implication the employment of probability analysis in the allocation of funds for dealing with threats to national security. Other agency members of the Strategic Materials Committee, including the State and Commerce departments, argued for a smaller stockpile on the grounds that larger purchases would generate inflation, but the proponents of a larger stockpile won. The JCS strategic assumptions were replaced by a formula known as the factoring system for judging the accessibility of supplies in wartime, the application of which resulted in a substantial increase in stockpile goals.

The Buy American provision in the 1946 act was also a source of controversy, particularly between the administration and Congress. On signing the 1946 stockpiling act, President Truman strongly objected to the Buy American provision. The general rule adopted by the administration was to favor domestic suppliers of commodities purchased for the stockpile if the domestic price was not more than 25 percent above the world price. This interpretation had no legislative basis. Since most materials purchased for the stockpile were not produced in the United States, however, the Buy American requirement was important in only a few cases.[10] More important for stimulating the domestic minerals industry were the purchase contracts under the Defense Production Act of 1950.

After the 1946 act was passed, building the stockpile took place slowly because of tight supply and market conditions in the immediate postwar period. Although a major purpose of the act was to reduce U.S. dependence on foreign nations for raw materials, the act also stated that purchases were to be made so far as practicable "from supplies of materials in excess of current industrial demand." The munitions board initially estimated that stockpile targets would total $2.1 billion, including some $300 million worth of materials to be transferred from wartime stocks held by the Reconstruction Finance

Corporation and other agencies; the balance of $1.8 billion was to be acquired over a five-year period. By the end of fiscal year 1950 the initial stockpile program was only about two-fifths complete. As a consequence of the rise in prices and changes in stockpile objectives, the munitions board raised the planned cost of the completed stockpile to $4.0 billion, of which $1.6 billion worth of materials was on hand.

After the outbreak of the Korean War in 1950, both Congress and the administration decided to accelerate stockpile acquisitions, and during the six months ending in January 1951 Congress appropriated $2.9 billion for stockpile purchases, more than three times the amount made available in the previous four years. The munitions board revised the stockpile objectives late in 1950, bringing the total valuation to $8.9 billion, some of the increase reflecting the rise in prices of materials. Government purchases for the stockpile were constrained, however, by increased private demand for materials and the accelerated armament program touched off by the Korean War.

The Defense Production Act and
Surplus Agricultural Commodities

The Defense Production Act of 1950 provided sweeping authority to expand both foreign and domestic production capacities and supplies and to allocate scarce materials among competing government programs and nondefense production. The act was administered by two newly created agencies, the Office of Defense Mobilization (ODM) and the Defense Production Administration (DPA). Stockpile acquisitions by the munitions board also came under the control of the ODM. The DPA negotiated contracts for the expansion of domestic and foreign production of minerals and either sold the materials acquired to private industry or to the strategic stockpile or held them. With the fulfillment of many contracts, the DPA inventory grew into a second stockpile of substantial size. DPA contracts for expanding production totaled $6.5 billion by March 31, 1953, and some of the output served to expand the strategic stockpile. The DPA also influenced the inventory objectives of the stockpiling program, which were changed to accommodate the aims of the ODM to expand domestic capacity.

During the first year of the Eisenhower administration (1953), the direction of stockpiling policy under the 1946 act was transferred from the munitions board (which was abolished) to the ODM. This move integrated stockpiling with other mobilization planning and operations under a civilian agency. The Department of Defense be-

14

came simply one of the advisory agencies in establishing stockpile goals. Moreover, since some of the materials contracted for by the DPA became part of the strategic stockpile inventory, these purchases had an important influence on the NDS program.

The congressional farm bloc viewed the stockpile program as a means of disposing of some of the surplus agricultural commodities arising from an agricultural price support program. The Agricultural Trade Development and Assistance Act of 1954 (Public Law 480) established a "supplemental stockpile" as a repository for strategic materials purchased with foreign currencies acquired by the sale of surplus agricultural commodities to developing countries. Materials in the supplemental stockpile were to be released only under the restrictions contained in the stockpiling act of 1946. The 1954 act also expanded the authority of the CCC to barter agricultural surpluses for strategic materials of foreign origin, and subsequent legislation provided for the transfer of barter acquisitions to the supplemental stockpile as well as to the strategic stockpile. Although no strategic materials were ever bought with foreign currency counterpart funds, the barter program acquired materials totaling $1.6 billion by 1967, when the last barter contract under the 1954 act was signed.[11] The inventory of the supplemental stockpile was later merged with the strategic stockpile.

Acquisitions under the Defense Production Act and the barter program were not necessarily in accordance with goals of the NDS program, but it is impossible to determine how far acquisitions of materials transferred from these programs have influenced NDS goals or have added to NDS inventories in excess of goals. There is evidence, however, that the ODM influenced NDS goals as well as acquisitions.

Setting Stockpile Goals: The Politics of Strategic Assessments

The multiple objectives of the NDS program complicated the development of a rational method of establishing stockpile goals. The initial goals based on the JCS strategic assumptions were objected to by the Department of the Interior, in part because they did not conform to the department's objective of promoting the expansion of domestic mineral-producing capacities. Because of this controversy and the change in strategic thinking brought about by the Korean War, a new method of calculating stockpile objectives was adopted, which substantially lowered the estimates of supplies available in wartime from overseas sources and therefore raised the stockpile goals. Beginning in 1950 the factoring system was used by the munitions board to determine materials and quantities for stockpile goals. Three objective criteria were used to determine the availability of supplies: military accessibility and shipping losses; political dependability of the source countries; and concentration of supply by region and total dependence on foreign sources. Countries judged by the JCS to be militarily inaccessible in time of general war were eliminated as a source of materials, and the normally available supplies from remaining sources were discounted to cover risks of shipping losses, political instability, and concentration of supply. An additional consideration was how essential each material was in the production process.

The stockpile goals were derived from four categories of assumptions (or estimates) about the war emergency during which the stockpiled materials would be released. These were the nature and duration of the war emergency; the accessibility of foreign sources of materials during the wartime emergency; the degree of austerity imposed on the civilian economy; and the total military and civilian demand for materials during a war emergency. Initially the first two categories were based on assessments by the JCS and the military agencies, but beginning in 1953 the ODM made the assessments with advice from the military. The other two categories were mainly the responsibility of the ODM and successor agencies, with advice from the Department of Defense on military requirements. Assumptions and estimates related to each of these categories have been changed from time to time as a consequence both of objective assessments and of political factors reflecting special economic interests.

The factoring system appeared to be more objective and precise than it actually was in its application. It left ample room for "intuitive judgments" based on prejudices and political considerations.[12] The decision to stockpile wool and long-staple cotton, for example, was influenced by farm state legislators, including Senator Lyndon B. Johnson of Texas, who headed the Preparedness Subcommittee of the Senate Commitee on Armed Services.[13] The factoring system was altered from time to time but remained the basic method of determining stockpile objectives until a somewhat more sophisticated method was adopted in 1976.

The War Scenarios

The initial war emergency scenario adopted by the JCS was a five-year war in which the entire Western Hemisphere and much of the Asia-Pacific and African regions would be accessible for materials. With the adoption of the factoring system in 1950, the accessibility of areas outside North America was substantially discounted. Despite changes in military technology, such as advances in nuclear weapons and intercontinental delivery capability by both the United States and the Soviet Union, the five-year-war scenario remained the strategic basis for stockpile goals until 1958, when it was reduced to three years.

The JCS had recommended this reduction as early as 1954, but it was strongly opposed by Arthur S. Flemming, director of the ODM. Flemming's position was supported by President Dwight D. Eisenhower even though the three-year-war planning period was favored by most other agencies concerned with the problem, including the Department of Defense, the Bureau of the Budget, and the Department of the Treasury. Flemming's position on the three- or five-year war issue was not based on his expertise as a military strategist but arose from his desire to expand stockpile purchases to assist the domestic mining industry. A reduction from five to three years would make the bulk of the stockpile inventory in excess of goals as they were calculated at the time. This situation not only would terminate most domestic stockpile purchases but in the eyes of Congress would reflect on the entire NDS program.

Eisenhower's support for a large stockpile and for the five-year-war assumption is more difficult to understand. A stockpile sufficient for a five-year war was clearly inconsistent with military planning during the late 1950s, which was based on a short nuclear war rather than a long conventional war.[14] Moreover, in the event of a large-scale nuclear war, the U.S. industrial base would be severely damaged and the requirements for strategic and critical materials thereby reduced. Thus a nuclear war would have to be fought primarily with equipment already produced and deployed at the outbreak. The National Security Council finally recommended the shift to a three-year war in 1958, and Eisenhower concurred. The effect was to reduce all stockpile objectives by 60 percent.[15]

In the 1960s the three-year-war assumption came increasingly under attack. Given the widespread expectation that any general war would be nuclear, the value of any strategic stockpile for use only in a global war was strongly questioned. On January 31, 1962, President Kennedy announced that in reviewing the stockpile program, "it was apparent to me that this excessive storage of costly materials was a questionable burden on public funds, and in addition the potential source of excessive and unconscionable profits." Kennedy also promised complete cooperation by the executive branch with the investigation initiated by the National Stockpile and Naval Petroleum Reserves Subcommittee under the chairmanship of Senator Stewart Symington. The draft report of the Symington subcommittee issued in October 1963 reached the following conclusion:

> Based on the testimony the Subcommittee concludes that the present stockpile assumption of a three-year conventional war is an anachronism, if not an absurdity. The NATO Alliance assumption for a conventional European war is one of 90 days duration; and there has been considerable discussion to reduce this to 30 days. It would appear that any realistic strategic planning for the stockpile ceased many years ago; and never advanced into the nuclear age as have other elements of the defense system of our country. Considering the constant peril this country faces from its enemies, the nation's security can no longer permit an important component part of its defenses to be outdated.[16]

Despite the misgivings of President Kennedy about the size of the stockpile and the conclusions of the Symington report, no basic change was made in the three-year-war planning assumption during either the Kennedy or the Johnson administration. Only small amounts were purchased for the stockpile during this period, and after the new strategic assumptions were adopted in 1958, the major problem was to dispose of excess inventories. Despite the disposal of $4.2 billion of stockpiled materials after 1958, excess inventories totaled $2.7 billion (market value) at the end of 1972.[17]

In April 1973 President Nixon announced new stockpile guidelines that would provide materials needed for the first year of a major conflict in Europe and Asia. He pointed out that, in the event of a long conflict, these "12 months would give us sufficient time to mobilize so that we could sustain our defense effort as long as necessary without placing an intolerable burden on the economy or the civilian population."[18] The Ford and Carter administrations returned to the three-year-war period as the basis for determining stockpile goals, and this policy has been continued by the Reagan administration.

Accessibility of Materials from Foreign Countries

Determining stockpile goals depends heavily on the accessibility of supplies from foreign countries, which depends on assessments of the nature of the war emergency, not simply its duration. Ideally, accessibility should have been determined by military strategists and political and economic specialists familiar with particular countries. This would need to be done for several war scenarios and the results combined into a range of probability coefficients for the reduction in

18

normal supplies for each imported material. The results could then have been used to determine either a single average estimated shortfall in foreign supplies or a maximum and minimum estimate. Although it is not known what methods were employed by the JCS, after the ODM assumed responsibility for establishing stockpile goals, estimates of availability from various foreign sources were made to fit the politically determined stockpile goals.

In 1954 the ODM and the Interior Department were anxious to increase purchases of lead and zinc for the stockpile to assist the domestic mining industry, but under the formula used by the previous administration, inventories of these commodities had already reached the goals. Therefore, the strategic assumptions about the availability of supplies from outside the United States and Canada were changed to create larger projected shortfalls in foreign supplies. These made it possible to justify increased stockpile acquisitions of lead and zinc and certain other domestically produced minerals.[19] To increase stockpile purchases of lead and zinc further, special long-term procurement goals above existing goals were established by the ODM in 1954, with the purchases confined to "newly mined metals and minerals of domestic origin."[20] One arbitrary aspect of the long-term goals was that the stockpile should contain at least one year's normal domestic consumption of any strategic material. This goal permitted the purchase of substantially larger amounts of both lead and zinc for the stockpile with no national security justification.[21] In addition, the base year from which requirements of zinc were projected was chosen to yield the highest possible consumption.

In his directive to the ODM to establish long-term stockpile objectives, President Eisenhower stated the following assumptions:

> 1. It will be assumed for the purpose of calculating long-term stockpile objectives that, in the event of war, supplies will not be available from foreign sources except in the case of that limited group of countries to which wartime access can be had with the same degree of reliance as afforded from sources within our country.
> 2. It will be assumed that in the event of an emergency some supplies from domestic sources may not be available, in view of the fact that the Soviets now have the capability of attack on the United States.[22]

This change in strategic assumptions differed radically from the factoring system based on discounts from normal availability from various areas of the world, including the Western Hemisphere outside North America. It is impossible to understand why Soviet bombing of the United States would reduce domestic supply of metals such as lead and zinc (to which the new policy was mainly directed) without at the same time reducing the productive facilities that use metals to manufacture military and civilian goods. All these devices to subvert the major purpose of the stockpile program and to assist domestic mining firms were brought out by the Symington subcommittee. Unfortunately, no basic reform of the program was instituted, nor did Congress undertake a serious reexamination of the rationale for the entire program or its contribution to national security.

A radical change in assumptions about the accessibility of foreign supplies in wartime was made by the Nixon administration. It assumed that some supplies would be available from countries outside America and the Caribbean in the event of a war emergency and that during the first year of a conflict the NDS, together with domestic production and assumed imports, would provide sufficient materials to support both national security and domestic needs without reducing the overall standard of living. If the conflict were to extend beyond one year, domestic austerity would be required to support critical defense needs. It was also expected that noncritical materials would be substituted for critical materials faster than assumed in the earlier projections.

The Nixon administration's April 1973 supply assumptions provided the basis for a proposed 90 percent reduction in the strategic stockpile, from $6.7 billion in April 1973 to about $700 million. The largest reductions were applied to domestically produced commodities such as aluminum, copper, lead, and zinc. On June 30, 1973, the General Services Administration (GSA) reduced stockpile objectives established under Eisenhower, creating an excess of about $4 billion in stockpile inventories.[23] During the Nixon administration Congress approved the disposal of $726 million worth of excess inventories.[24]

New Guidelines Established by the
Ford and Carter Administrations

President Nixon's stockpile program was strongly criticized both in and outside the government. In a review of the reduction in stockpile goals in 1975, the General Accounting Office (GAO) criticized the new policy both because it found the change in strategic assumptions arbitrary and subjective and because the program failed to take into account the growing world demand for materials in relation to the growth in supplies and the possibility of disruptions of supply arising from embargoes and cartels. The GAO report was influenced by the 1973–1974 Arab oil embargo and OPEC price increase and by the several-fold increase by some bauxite-producing countries of export taxes on bauxite.[25] Such contingencies occurred during peacetime, however, and had nothing to do with supply conditions during a major war.

On the basis of recommendations made by an interagency committee, in the fall of 1976 President Gerald Ford issued the following policy guidelines for the NDS program:

• Planning would be based on a three-year war emergency with flexible goals for individual materials.

• Materials required for a wartime emergency would be divided into three categories: defense, essential civilian, and general civilian, with requirements estimated separately under different criteria and for each year of an assumed war.

• Estimates of supplies and requirements and of the resulting stockpile goals would be prepared and reviewed by an interagency committee.

• The goals were to be viewed as long-range targets toward which progress would be made and could be revised to reflect changing technological and strategic circumstances.[26]

The new goals took into account both civilian and defense needs and called for a several-fold increase in the total value of stockpile inventories over those set by the Nixon administration. Greater emphasis was put, however, on stockpiling materials for which the United States depended heavily on foreign sources than on purchases that would benefit the domestic mining industry, as the Eisenhower goals had done. President Ford's January 1977 budget provided for purchases of stockpile materials in line with these policy goals, but the Carter administration declared a moratorium on both sales and purchases of stockpile materials until the entire stockpile issue could be reviewed by another interagency committee.

In September 1977 President Jimmy Carter issued new stockpile guidelines that accepted the Ford guidelines with one major amendment: higher priority was to be given to the *preparation* for a one-year NATO war in Europe with no more than thirty days' warning than to meeting requirements during any of the three years of a conventional war. Presumably special strategic assumptions were to be applied to the accessibility of materials and requirements before the first year of a NATO war in Europe. But it is difficult to understand the role of the stockpile in preparing to fight a war on short notice. What are needed for this purpose are quantities of military equipment in place—not raw materials. In fact, it is doubtful whether anything would be used during the first year of a war that had not already been manufactured before the war began.

Legislative Proposals for Revising the 1946 Stockpiling Act

Bills were introduced in 1977 to revise the 1946 stockpiling act, two of which were broadly in line with the Carter guidelines (H.R. 4895 and S. 1198) while a third (S. 1810) would require stockpile quantities to be determined on the basis of the quantity of each material imported each year. S. 1810, introduced by Senator James McClure of Idaho, had the backing of the American Mining Congress but was vigorously opposed by the administration. The mining industry was concerned that changes in stockpile goals and subsequent disposal of excess inventories would harm it.[27] It therefore preferred a simple method of determining the quantities to be acquired. Administration spokesmen argued that this so-called import dependency approach failed to take into account the different requirements for individual materials in peacetime and for wartime.

Congress was slow to act on a new stockpiling bill, and a number of changes were made in the initial bills that were generally consistent with the Ford-Carter guidelines. The congressional committees were particularly concerned with the ultimate cost of achieving stockpile goals, but since those goals not only were flexible and long term but were defined in terms of commodities whose prices changed from time to time, the ultimate cost was a matter of conjecture. Moreover, since purchases for the stockpile were authorized annually and a substantial portion of the purchases could be financed by the disposal of excess inventories, Congress had full control over the stockpile budget.

Nevertheless, questions were raised, particularly by Senator William Proxmire of Wisconsin, about the cost of the program. Proxmire suggested an amendment to H.R. 2154, the Strategic and Critical Materials Stockpiling Revision Act of 1979, that would have limited the stockpile to military and essential civilian requirements and eliminated goals designed to maintain civilian consumption in wartime. This would have reduced the estimated cost of the 1979 goals from $11.6 billion (in 1977 prices) to $5.3 billion.[28] Proxmire's skepticism about the Ford-Carter guidelines and the probability of a three-year conventional war was indicated in his statement that "the remote possibility of our involvement in such a conflict and the limited national security advantages of guaranteeing a certain level of nonessential civilian consumption do not justify a $6.3 billion increase in stockpile expenditures."[29]

Proxmire's amendment was rejected by administration officials on the grounds that "the United States could not fight an extended conventional war without a strong civilian economy." Moreover, they argued that a sharp separation between civilian and defense material requirements and facilities was impossible.[30] This criticism of Proxmire's amendment appears valid only if the three-year conventional war scenario is fully accepted. Actually, Proxmire was seeking to reduce the proposed large outlay for an unlikely contingency. In a hearing before the Senate Committee on Banking, Housing, and Urban Affairs, which he chaired, Senator Proxmire criticized the assumptions underlying the Carter stockpile guidelines. He pointed out that "reliance on the World War II scenario borders on the absurd. Why are we stockpiling for this age-worn contingency when logic points us in another direction?" He questioned why, even if the assumption of a three-year major war was realistic, the strategic stockpile was geared to that contingency while other components of U.S. national security were not. Proxmire questioned whether an increased expenditure of $4 to $8 billion on the strategic stockpile constituted the best allocation of the limited resources available for security. Moreover, if this expenditure could be justified, "one must explain how we can afford, from a national security standpoint, to delay fulfillment of stockpile goals for 15 to 20 years. To argue the national security need on the one hand, and to delay the acquisition of materials on the other, strikes me as highly inconsistent."[31]

Proxmire pointed out that during the Ford administration's review of stockpile policy, the Office of Management and Budget, the Department of the Treasury, and the Council on International Economic Policy all recommended against stockpiling for nonessential civilian consumption, which constituted 55 percent of the estimated value of stockpile goals in 1978.[32] Testimony during the hearings revealed that current U.S. and NATO defense planning was geared to a short war with little or no warning before the outbreak of war, which appeared to Proxmire to contradict the assumptions of the Carter stockpile guidelines.[33] Finally, Proxmire was concerned that the stockpile would be used to support private domestic mining interests or for other economic purposes not related to national security. Proxmire proposed amendments to the stockpile bills (H.R. 2154 and S. 290) designed to limit the goals and to prevent the use of the program for purposes other than security, but his amendments were rejected.

Government Interest in Economic Stockpiling

Although U.S. stockpile legislation has been mainly directed to maintaining the availability of strategic minerals during a major war, there has been interest in and outside the government in protecting the general economy from the effects of disruptions of supplies in peace-time. This interest was particularly strong after the 1973–1974 Arab oil embargo, when there was widespread concern that foreign cartels or embargoes would create shortages and high prices of other imported minerals, such as bauxite. Under the 1946 stockpiling act certain metals were released from the NDS for the civilian economy in periods of high prices. These sales were criticized as contrary to the purposes of that act, and domestic producers of the metals opposed them. One reason most congressmen favored limiting disposals from the NDS to periods of war emergency was their desire to avoid using the program to stabilize prices of domestically produced materials. The function of an economic stockpile, however, is to reduce the economic effect of import disruptions resulting from abnormal noneconomic events abroad, such as cartels, embargoes, civil disturbances in major producing areas, and regional wars. It is not expected to offset price movements arising from normal market forces.

In 1975 two economic stockpile bills were introduced in the Ninety-fourth Congress, one (S. 1869) by Senator Harrison Williams on June 4 and the other (H.R. 9597) by Representatives Thomas Rees and J. William Stanton on September 11. The Williams bill was a simple amendment to the Defense Production Act of 1950 providing authority for the establishment of an economic stockpile without details; the Rees-Stanton bill (called the National Economic Stockpiling Association Act) would have established a public-private association for the purchase and sale of raw materials.

Neither bill was acted on by congressional committees, but in June 1976 the Subcommittee on Materials Availability of the House Committee on Defense Production held hearings on the purpose and organization of economic stockpiling.[34] Although no specific economic stockpiling bill was considered in these hearings, several nongovernmental witnesses, including C. Fred Bergsten of the Brookings Institution and Timothy Stanley of the International Economic Policy Association, testified in favor of an economic stockpile program, and government witnesses expressed varying degrees of sympathy with the idea or criticism of it.[35] Simon D. Strauss testified on behalf of the American Mining Congress that the mining industry did not support economic stockpiling and believed that any economic stockpiles created should be limited to products for which the United States depends heavily on imports.[36] Congressional interest was indicated by the publication of a study on economic stockpiling by the Office of Technology Assessment at the request of the House Committee on Science and Technology.[37]

President Carter was also concerned about the effect of disruptions of foreign supply on the U.S. economy during peacetime. In April 1977 he stated that his administration would "work with Congress to assure that raw materials from our strategic stockpiles are available to meet supply disruptions during peacetime and to aid industry in evaluating future market conditions. These efforts should exclude the use of the strategic stockpile for purposes of general price stabilization."[38] The president may have been influenced in making this statement by the December 1976 report to the president and the Congress by the National Commission on Supplies and Shortages. The commission recommended that the 1946 stockpiling act be amended to "permit the use of the strategic stockpile in the event of a severe disruption in the supply of a critical material, and that the President be required to issue rules for such contingencies." As an alternative the commission recommended that a separate, limited economic stockpile be established but that "Congress explicitly prohibit the use of any public stockpile to subsidize a domestic industry or to influence domestic prices in the absence of an actual or threatened supply disruption."[39] I am not aware of any initiatives taken by the Carter administration either to make stockpile materials subject to disruption available in peacetime to the civilian economy or to establish an economic stockpile.

Many of the arguments for increasing NDS inventories found in congressional hearings and in private publications refer to the vulnerability of the U.S. economy to disruptions of supplies of strategic materials, such as chromium, cobalt, and manganese, from Africa and other areas subject to political instability. Yet, according to law, materials from the NDS cannot be made available in peacetime to nondefense industries in the event of such contingencies. The NDS program is simply not designed to deal with supply disruptions of this kind, which would be the major function of an economic stockpile. It seems questionable whether some supporters of a larger strategic stockpile fully understand the limitations of the present NDS program.

Strategic and Materials Stockpiling Act of 1979

The 1979 stockpiling act generally followed the Ford-Carter guidelines and differed from the 1946 act in several important ways. First, stockpile acquisitions are to be used solely to promote national security and not to assist domestic industries, control commodity prices, or generate receipts for budgetary purposes. Second, competitive procedures are to be used in acquiring and disposing of materials, and no mention is made of giving preference to domestic pro-

ducers in accordance with the Buy American Act of 1933. Third, stockpile goals are to be designed to sustain the United States for not less than three years in a war emergency.

Fourth, to stabilize the stockpile goals, the act provides that goals may not be revised unless the Committees on Armed Services of the Senate and the House are notified at least thirty days before the effective date and retains the provisions in the 1946 act that require authorization before any excess inventory is released from the stockpile. It also requires that acquisitions of materials be authorized, except that acquisition authority is by lump-sum amount because of the market's sensitivity to commodity-quantity information. Exceptions are granted for transactions involving processing, refining, or upgrading existing stocks or for the rotation of stocks.

Fifth, the act provides that the president may order the release of stockpile materials at any time he "determines the release of such materials is required for purposes of the national defense; and in time of war declared by the Congress or during a national emergency." Finally, receipts from the sale of excess materials are to be placed in a National Defense Stockpile Transactions Fund (NDSTF), to be used only to acquire new materials. A sunset provision transferring unappropriated funds to the Treasury at the end of three fiscal years and appropriated funds at the end of five fiscal years prevents indefinite tying up of funds.

The 1979 act combined materials accumulated under the Defense Production Act of 1950 and those accumulated under barter and other programs with the NDS. The act continues the barter program, but the stockpile program could presumably not be manipulated to dispose of surplus agricultural commodities. The question of the desirability of the barter program is discussed in chapter 3.

The 1979 act left the managerial organization of the stockpile program to the president but set forth guidelines for acquisition and disposal, some of which are noted above. An executive order of July 15, 1979, assigned stockpiling activities to the Federal Emergency Management Agency (FEMA), which, in conjunction with a complex system of governmental committees, establishes stockpile goals and the Annual Materials Plan (AMP). The AMP is a list of stockpile materials for acquisition and disposal that is submitted to Congress as part of the president's annual budget. The management functions for the stockpile, including buying and selling materials, storage, rotation, and financing for processing materials, were delegated to the GSA.

In his April 1982 report to Congress on the National Materials and Minerals Program Plan, President Reagan endorsed the stockpile policies set forth in the 1979 stockpiling act and the Ford-Carter guidelines and proposed no substantive changes.[40] On July 8, 1985, however, the White House announced that President Reagan was proposing a substantial change in both the stockpile goals and the criteria and methods for determining the goals. Although details were not revealed in this announcement, the stockpile for the forty-two most significant materials currently in the stockpile would contain materials valued at $6.7 billion, as contrasted with stockpile goals valued at $16.3 billion (in May 1985 prices) under the existing program. The new stockpile goals would eliminate $9.7 billion in unmet goals under the existing program and leave $3.2 billion as surplus materials above the new goals, of which $2.5 billion would be sold over the next five years. Receipts from the sales would go to fill unmet materials goals, including any goals that may result from analyses of the twenty materials yet to be studied, with the remainder used to reduce the federal budget deficit. Despite the proposed 59 percent reduction in stockpile goals, the White House announcement stated that the revised goals "will be sufficient to meet military, industrial and essential civilian needs for a three-year conventional global military conflict, as mandated by Congress in 1979."[41] According to the president's proposal, inventories of strategic materials valued at only $0.7 billion (tier I) would be required during a protracted military conflict for supplementing materials not available in sufficient quantities from domestic or reliable foreign sources. The stockpile would, however, contain a "supplementary reserve" of materials (tier II) currently valued at $6 billion.

Legislative Activity on Stockpiling after 1979

Only minor amendments were made to the 1979 stockpiling act after July 1979, but several bills were introduced to alter the character of the NDS program.[42] One bill (S. 1982) would have created an independent stockpiling commission similar to the Federal Reserve Board, which would have complete jurisdiction over the NDS program and the materials purchasing and contracting authority under Title III of the Defense Production Act of 1950.[43] One purpose of the bill was to make it easier to acquire materials for the stockpile more rapidly, but another obvious purpose was to use the program to promote the domestic production of minerals, such as cobalt and copper, by negotiating contracts under the Defense Production Act for materials to be delivered to the stockpile. In June 1981 the Subcommittee on Preparedness of the Senate Armed Services Committee held hearings on S. 1228, a bill to prescribe a method for determining the quantity of material to be stockpiled based on import dependency. This bill was similar to that introduced by Senator McClure (S. 1810) in 1977 and strongly supported by the American Mining Congress. These and other bills, including one introduced in December 1982 (H.R. 7414) proposing to transfer the management of the NDS to the secretary of defense, were not acted on by Congress.

In 1982 and 1983 several bills were introduced to provide funding for government purchases of domestic materials under Title III of the Defense Production Act of 1950. Such legislation would have affected the NDS program since it provided for stockpile acquisition of government-subsidized production. Supporters of the program, including the American Mining Congress and some U.S. government officials, argued that domestic production would reduce the amount of materials needed to be held in the stockpile. Subsidizing domestic production of minerals as an alternative to stockpiling is discussed in chapter 5.

Notes

1. No comprehensive history of the NDS program has been published. An excellent study by Glenn H. Snyder, *Stockpiling Strategic Materials: Politics and National Defense* (San Francisco: Chandler Publishing, 1966), covers the period 1946–1964. A paper by David E. Lockwood, "The Stockpiling of Strategic and Critical Materials" (Washington, D.C.: Congressional Research Service, Library of Congress, May 1974, processed), summarizes the legislative history over the period 1939–1973. In preparing this chapter, I have drawn on these two sources plus congressional hearings and reports and publications of the Federal Emergency Management Agency.

2. The first legislative measure creating a strategic materials reserve was the Naval Appropriations Act of 1937, which granted authority for the purchase of $3.5 million worth of materials during fiscal 1938.

3. This discussion of the debates leading to passage of the 1946 Strategic and Critical Materials Stock Piling Act draws heavily on Synder, *Stockpiling Strategic Materials*, chap. 1.

4. S. 1160, 78th Congress, 1st session.

5. Glenn Snyder stated that an organizational chart of the administrative machinery of the stockpile program resembled a "Rube Goldberg cartoon of a contraption performing an essentially simple operation by an amazingly complicated process." Snyder, *Stockpiling Strategic Materials*, p. 35.

6. During the Eisenhower administration stockpile purchases of lead and zinc were manipulated to raise the prices of these metals. Ibid., pp. 199–209.

7. Ibid., p. 107.

8. Ibid., p. 109.

9. Ibid., p. 110.

10. Ibid., p. 81.

11. In 1983 the CCC bartered agricultural commodities for 1 million tons of

Jamaican bauxite. Federal Emergency Management Agency, *Stockpile Report to the Congress, April–September 1983* (Washington, D.C., April 1984), p. 1.

12. Snyder, *Stockpiling Strategic Materials*, pp. 132–36.

13. Ibid., p. 136.

14. Ibid., pp. 229–31. See also Samuel P. Huntington, *The Common Defense: Strategic Programs in National Politics* (New York: Columbia University Press, 1961), p. 97.

15. The 60 percent decrease reflected the fact that military plans under the five-year program called for a rising curve of requirements reaching a peak in the third year. Huntington, *The Common Defense*.

16. U.S. Congress, Senate, Committee on Armed Services, Subcommittee on National Stockpile and Naval Petroleum Reserves, *Inquiry into the Strategic and Critical Materials Stockpiles of the United States* (draft report), 88th Congress, 1st session, p. 108. No final report was ever issued, because of a conflict within the subcommittee.

17. Office of Emergency Preparedness, *Stockpile Report to the Congress, July–December 1972* (Washington, D.C., 1973), p. 2. One of the reasons for the continued high excess inventories despite large disposals was the increase in prices of the materials.

18. White House, *Special Message to the Congress Proposing Disposal Legislation* (Washington, D.C., April 16, 1973). In reducing the size of the stockpile, President Nixon was motivated by a desire to reduce inflation and the budgetary deficit. Because the early 1970s were a period of high metal prices, there was little pressure to assist domestic minerals industries.

19. Snyder, *Stockpiling Strategic Materials*, pp. 194–97. See also Senate, Subcommittee on National Stockpile, *Inquiry*, pp. 21–22.

20. White House, *Press Release* (Washington, D.C., March 26, 1954). See also Snyder, *Stockpiling Strategic Materials*, p. 195. One reason given for Eisenhower's decision was that he had just rejected the recommendation of the U.S. Tariff Commission to increase tariffs on lead and zinc.

21. See Senate, Subcommittee on National Stockpile, *Inquiry*, p. 22.

22. White House, *Press Release*.

23. See General Accounting Office, "Stockpile Objectives of Strategic and Critical Materials Should Be Reconsidered because of Shortages" (Washington, D.C., March 11, 1975, processed), pp. i–ii. Responsibility for the stockpile program was transferred from the ODM to the GSA during the Nixon administration.

24. Ibid.

25. Ibid., pp. 6–8.

26. U.S. Congress, Joint Committee on Defense Production, *Hearings, Defense Industrial Base: New Stockpile Objectives*, 94th Congress, 2d session, November 24, 1976, pp. 3–15.

27. See statement by Simon D. Strauss on behalf of the American Mining Congress, U.S. Congress, Senate, Committee on Armed Services, Subcommittee on Military Construction and Stockpiles, *Hearings, General Stockpile Policy*, 95th Congress, 1st session, September 9, 1977, pp. 60–64.

28. U.S. Congress, House, Committee on Armed Services, Subcommittee

on Seapower and Strategic and Critical Materials, *Hearings on H.R. 2154*, 96th Congress, 1st session, February 23, 1979, pp. 33–38. H.R. 2154 evolved from H.R. 4895, which passed the House; the identical bill, S. 1198, did not pass the Senate.

29. Ibid., p. 34.

30. Ibid., p. 32. Criticisms of Proxmire's amendments were given by Joseph A. Mitchell, director, Federal Preparedness Agency, GSA.

31. U.S. Congress, Senate, Committee on Banking, Housing, and Urban Affairs, *Hearings, Strategic Stockpile Policy*, 95th Congress, 2d session, November 14, 1978, pp. 1–3.

32. Ibid., p. 3.

33. Ibid., p. 108.

34. U.S. Congress, House, Joint Committee on Defense Production, Subcommittee on Materials Availability, *Hearings, Purpose and Organization of Economic Stockpiling*, 94th Congress, 2d session, June 8–9, 1976.

35. Ibid.

36. Ibid., pp. 29–32.

37. Office of Technology Assessment, *An Assessment of Alternative Economic Stockpiling Practices* (Washington, D.C., August 1976).

38. Quoted in A. Jordan and R. Kilmarx, *Strategic Minerals Dependence: The Stockpile Dilemma*, Washington Papers (Beverly Hills, Calif.: Sage Publications, 1979), p. 65.

39. National Commission on Supplies and Shortages, *Government and the Nation's Resources* (Washington, D.C., December 1976), p. xvii.

40. White House, *National Materials and Minerals Program Plan and Report to Congress* (Washington, D.C., April 5, 1982).

41. White House, "National Defense Stockpile Policy," *Press Release*, July 8, 1985.

42. The Omnibus Budget Reconciliation Act of 1981 (Public Law 97-35) removed the five-year limit on the use of appropriated funds in the National Defense Stockpile Transactions Fund; the requirement that funds revert to the Treasury after three years if not appropriated was also deleted. A limit of $1 billion was placed on the funds to be held in the NDSTF until September 30, 1983, when the limit became $500 million.

43. U.S. Congress, Senate, Committee on Armed Services, Subcommittee on Preparedness, *Hearings on S. 1982 and S. 2429*, 97th Congress, 2d session, June 9–10, 1982, pp. 2–53.

3
National Defense Stockpile: Organization, Policies, and Programs

The principal functions of the NDS program are to determine stockpile goals in accordance with guidelines established by Congress and the president and to prepare the Annual Materials Plan (AMP) for acquisition and disposal of stockpile inventory for each fiscal year, together with estimates for the following four years. Since the stockpile goals for individual commodities usually require a number of years to fulfill and are revised from time to time, the AMP is the more important policy function. It is submitted to Congress for authorization and appropriation of funds.

Preparation of both stockpile goals and the AMP is initiated and coordinated by the Federal Emergency Management Agency (FEMA). A number of interagency committees develop estimates and review policy. The complex organization is not detailed here, because it is frequently changed by executive order and because shifts in organizational structure do not reveal policy changes. This chapter is mainly concerned with the methods of determining stockpile goals and the process of preparing the AMP.

Determining Stockpile Goals

The methods of determining stockpile objectives during the early years of the 1946 stockpiling act were quite crude, and the strategic assumptions were frequently changed. The nature of the potential war was poorly defined, and the definition was altered from time to time. This alteration led to changes in judgments about the accessibility of supplies from various areas of the world. Materials requirements were divided into those needed for production of military goods and services and those needed for essential civilian production, including production for export. Essential civilian requirements were initially calculated from the average civilian consumption for the 1942–1944 period, adjusted for population growth and changes in technology. The methods of estimating both requirements and supplies became increasingly sophisticated. Beginning in the early 1970s computerized models were developed for estimating material requirements during a simulated war emergency. A more rational method was also employed for estimating domestic and foreign supplies.

In 1976 a new procedure for determining stockpile goals, which has been continued with relatively minor changes, was adopted.[1] It was first applied in preparing the stockpile goals announced on October 1, 1976. The new goals for a number of materials were substantially larger than the stockpile objectives published immediately before October 1, 1976, and goals for additional commodities were added. These changes reflected both the new guidelines set forth by President Ford and the new method of determining goals employed by FEMA.[2] The goals for the alumina-aluminum group, the chromium group, the platinum-group metals, lead, manganese, tungsten, and zinc, among others, were substantially increased. Since stockpile inventories had increased little since 1959, the larger goals substantially reduced the excess inventories held by FEMA and increased the additional expenditures required for some materials not in the inventory.

The October 1976 goals remained in effect with few changes until April 1980, when new goals were announced. The total value of the 1980 goals was $18.7 billion, an increase of about 1.5 percent from the October 1976 goals (both in 1979 prices).[3] Except for eliminating a few nonmetallic items, such as castor oil, feathers and down, and opium, only minor changes were made in stockpile goals between 1980 and March 1984.[4]

Stockpile goals are designed to cover differences between projected requirements and projected supplies of strategic materials during a future war. In 1984 essentially two war scenarios were used in the planning process—a conventional NATO war with a short warning period and a three-year, two-front conventional war with a one-year warning period.[5] These scenarios are basically the same as those outlined in the Carter guidelines set forth in September 1977.

Method of Estimating Strategic Material Requirements. Estimating requirements of strategic materials for a three-year war begins with a macroeconomic forecast of the economy under peacetime conditions for a three-year period in the future. This baseline forecast is then adjusted by applying wartime planning factors affecting real expenditures for consumption, investment, government, exports, and imports—the five categories that determine final demand for the gross national product. The application of wartime planning factors—taxation, monetary policy, government expenditures, and direct controls—will have effects on the economy that must be taken into account in determining the economic variables in each of the three years of the hypothetical war.

The strategic materials examined for possible inclusion in the stockpile are used to produce goods and services in the economy.[6] The amount of each of these materials required to produce the output of each economic sector or industry is determined through a specially designed input-output table that includes the domestic industries producing strategic materials and converts the dollar figures used in the Department of Commerce input-output table into physical units.[7] From this input-output analysis material consumption ratios (MCRs) for each material by industry and by year are calculated by dividing consumption estimates by the corresponding industry output. As technology changes, however, the MCRs change from year to year, and it is also possible by substituting more abundant for less abundant materials to change the MCRs during the war period. The total amount of each strategic material required for each of the war years can be determined by multiplying the projections of each industry's output for each war year by the corresponding MCRs for each strategic material.[8]

Since the U.S. economy expands every year and changes occur in technology, in the product composition of the GNP, and in weapons systems and defense requirements, projected materials requirements for the war period must be continuously altered. For these reasons as well as changes in the outlook for material supplies, stockpile goals must be adjusted accordingly. Thus the goals are not planned commitments to purchase specific quantities for the stockpile but are regarded as flexible targets that depend on policy guidelines and dynamic economic, strategic, technological, and political factors.

To estimate materials requirements in each year of the war period, the economy is divided into three tiers—defense, essential civilian, and basic industrial (formerly general civilian)—and separate sets of requirements are estimated for each tier in each war year.[9] Special requirements are calculated for the first year of a NATO war with a short warning.

The defense tier includes all production necessary to obtain weapons, manpower, and support, including production necessary to support suppliers of defense contractors. The essential civilian tier includes those goods and services necessary to ensure the health, morale, and safety of the civilian population. It includes expenditures for food, shelter, clothing, and essential transportation. The basic industrial tier includes other goods and services consumed by the civilian population and deemed necessary to maintain a viable industrial base in support of the defense effort.[10]

Consumption and investment in the third tier would be subject to wartime planning factors that include macroeconomic policies, such as monetary and fiscal policies, selective credit controls, price controls, direct controls over investment, resource allocations (including materials allocation), and rationing. There would also be foreign trade controls and manpower allocations. These economic controls would reduce production of consumer durables and housing, together with investment in manufacturing plant and equipment for the production of less essential civilian goods. The objective would be to redirect economic resources to meet defense requirements and essential civilian needs.

Estimating Supplies of Strategic Materials

In projecting estimates of supplies of strategic materials for each year of the war planning period, the most difficult problem is to estimate the reliability of various foreign sources for each material. Such estimates must be based on strategic assumptions for the war scenario, the details of which are secret. The Bureau of Mines and the Bureau of Domestic Commerce prepare projections of global supplies from all domestic and foreign sources in the absence of war, together with possibilities of expanded production by those sources in response to increased demand. A factoring process is applied to these estimates to determine the degree of accessibility of each foreign source in the war period. First the strategic assumptions eliminate countries in zones of war action. Next, the remaining supplier countries are rated for political reliability on the following major factors: political orientation toward the United States; ability to sustain exports of stockpile materials in wartime; dependability of the labor force in wartime; and vulnerability to sabotage. The major factors are assigned weights, and the scores are combined into an index for each country. These ratings are made by State Department desk officers, and the indexes are evaluated by other State Department officials.

Countries ranked below a certain probability percentile of a normal (bell-shaped) distribution are not considered reliable sources of supply; countries above this percentile are acceptable for purposes of the industrial base tier. Only countries ranked above a substantially higher probability percentile are acceptable as sources for the essential civilian tier; and only countries ranked above, say, the ninetieth percentile are acceptable as supply sources for the defense tier.[11] Only Canada is considered an assured supplier. After the countries are ranked, estimates of transportation losses are applied to supplies from each foreign source.

Separate estimates of supplies are made for each tier and for each war year. The differences between the estimates and the requirements for the corresponding tier become the basis for establishing stockpile goals for the tier. As noted above, however, the supply estimates are based for the defense sector on availability from foreign sources subject to a very low risk, for the essential civilian sector on sources subject to a moderate risk, and for the basic industrial sector on sources subject to greater risk. In addition:

> Each tier supports the tier or tiers above it for any given material. If there is a wartime shortage for a stockpile material for the defense tier, then stockpile inventory is diverted from that amount set aside for the basic industrial tier, and, if this is not available, from the material held for the essential civilian tier.[12]

This scheme also provides the basis for priorities in procurement for the stockpile in the AMP. Thus the highest priority is given to procurement of materials for the stockpile for the defense sector for the first year of a NATO war with little warning. Second priority would presumably be given to materials required for the defense tier on the assumption of a three-year, two-front conventional war with one year's warning. Five priority classifications in all apply to both stockpile goals and annual procurement.[13]

An unadjusted stockpile goal for a given material is calculated by summing imbalances among the nine possibilities in the three-year, three-tier combination. Unadjusted goals are then evaluated in light of "special materials" criteria that take account of circumstances related to individual materials. These circumstances may have to do with the percentage of end uses of the material for defense or the degree of dependence of the stockpile material on imports from outside North America.

The forms in which stockpile materials are held depend on processing capacity in the United States. If that capacity is insufficient to process a material in its basic form, such as ore, some of the material is held in an upgraded form. For example, because U.S. alumina-producing capacity is not sufficient to process all the bauxite needed for the estimated requirements for aluminum, some of the stockpile may be held as alumina or aluminum.[14]

The Annual Materials Plan

The AMP process is initiated by FEMA, which prepares a list of stockpile goals for each material, together with shortfalls or overages between existing inventories and goals, and the priorities for acquiring materials for the stockpile. On March 31, 1984, the aggregate value of the goals was $17.3 billion, of which inventory held was valued at $7.1 billion and the additional amount required to fill the goals at $10.2 billion (all in March 1984 prices). The value of the existing inventory was $10.9 billion, of which $3.8 billion was in excess of goals.

The AMP provides for acquisitions and disposals for the stockpile for the next fiscal year, both of which must be acted on by Congress. The initial program prepared by FEMA is subject to review and amendment by a complex system of interagency committees coordinated by the AMP steering committee, chaired by FEMA. The actual quantities of commodities to be acquired or disposed of are proposed by the GSA after it evaluates the market outlook and transmitted to two subcommittees, the Strategic Implications Subcommittee, chaired by the Department of Defense, and the Market and International Political Impact Subcommittee, cochaired by the Departments of Commerce and State. The analyses undertaken by these subcommittees are presented to the AMP steering committee, which prepares a recommended AMP that is submitted to the director of FEMA for approval and to the National Security Council for review. The final AMP is submitted to the House and Senate Armed Services committees.

During the review process the proposals are examined in relation to anticipated changes in defense requirements. They are also evaluated from the standpoint of their effects on domestic and international commodity markets and their international economic and political effects, such as how proposed disposals might affect the earnings of foreign producer countries.

In recent years acquisitions have been financed from the NDSTF, and there is a relation between disposals that contribute to the fund and the money available for acquisitions. Thus the AMP for fiscal year 1985 totaled $120 million and was predicated on receipts from the disposal of eighteen materials held in excess of goals, including a substantial amount of silver for which authorization for disposal was withheld by Congress.[15] The Department of Defense Authorization Act of 1985 (Public Law 98–525) limited the balance in the NDSTF to $250 million to speed up procurement. In early 1985, however, the administration halted purchases of materials for the stockpile until completion and approval of the stockpile report by the National Security Council. As a consequence, sales of excess stockpile materials had to be curtailed to prevent the balance from rising above the $250 million limit.

Materials for the stockpile may also be acquired by barter of surplus agricultural and other surplus commodities held by the government for strategic materials. For sixteen years before 1983, barter had not been used to acquire stockpile materials. In 1983 and 1984, however, 1.4 million tons of Jamaican bauxite were contracted for by barter of surplus agricultural commodities.

Conditions for Release of Stockpile Materials

The 1979 stockpiling act authorized the president to release stockpile materials in time of war or during a national emergency or at any time he determines that releases are required for national defense. The authority to release materials under conditions short of war or other national emergency has been interpreted to mean that releases can be made to keep defense production moving, provided that it can be shown that the material to meet defense requirements is unavailable in the domestic market and that a redistribution of materials currently in the market to meet requirements for national defense would cause hardship to essential civilian production.[16] Although any released material must be used directly to support production for defense, the total available to the economy would be increased whenever a release occurred since civilian producers would presumably be able to obtain more of the nonstockpiled material in the market. This authority has been used only rarely in recent years.[17] Apparently the possibility of such releases is not taken into account in determining stockpile goals. Nevertheless, it is conceivable that a peacetime disruption of supplies of cobalt or chromium from Africa that continued for two or more years would significantly reduce the stockpile inventories of those commodities, so that they would be insufficient to meet calculated three-year-war requirements.

Summary of the NDS Program

The long-run stockpile goals and the annual adjustments of inventories are oriented to two rigidly specified war scenarios—a conventional NATO war with little warning and a three-year, two-front war with one year's warning. To determine the strategic mineral requirements for the three-year-war period, a planned domestic economy with income distribution, production, investment, and consumption modeled by a complex of macroeconomic and direct controls is projected. Foreign supplies of strategic materials during the war period are estimated on a basis of strategic assumptions within the framework of the war scenario. The stockpile goals are derived by totaling imbalances between requirements and supplies for the defense, essential civilian, and industrial base tiers into which the economy is divided. Markets and competitive prices play little role in allocating resources in this model war economy.

Although the war period may occur at any time, the strategic goals are long-run targets subject to change. It will require many years of annual incremental changes in the inventories before the goals can be achieved. Given the flexibility of the goals, they may never be approximated. All this takes place in the context of a highly dynamic domestic economy, rapidly changing weapons systems and military strategies, and a dynamic economic, political, and military world environment.

It may be noted that if the new stockpile goals proposed by President Reagan in July 1985 are adopted, the problem of matching stockpile goals to inventories will to a large degree be eliminated. Although some additions to stockpile inventories will evidently be required to meet the tier I goals valued at $0.7 billion, the supplemental reserve (tier II) valued at $6.0 billion is already in the stockpile inventory. It is interesting to note that President Nixon's basic stockpile requirement was also set at $0.7 billion. By classifying the additional $6.0 billion in existing stockpile inventories as a supplemental reserve, President Reagan's proposal avoids creating a very large excess inventory that would presumably need to be liquidated.

Notes

1. FEMA has never published a detailed exposition of the methods used to set stockpile goals. The description in this study is based on several unpublished memorandums originating in FEMA, public addresses, congressional testimony by FEMA officials, and FEMA's semiannual *Stockpile Report to the Congress*.

2. In October 1976 the term "stockpile goals" was substituted for "stockpile objectives." For a comparison of the October 1, 1976, stockpile goals with the stockpile objectives for September 1976, see Federal Preparedness Agency, *Stockpile Report to the Congress, July–September 1976* (Washington, D.C., March 1977), pp. 4–7, 17–19.

3. Federal Emergency Management Agency, *Stockpile Report to the Congress, October 1979–March 1980* (Washington, D.C., April 1980).

4. Federal Emergency Management Agency, *Stockpile Report to the Congress, October 1983–March 1984* (Washington, D.C., April 1984), and earlier issues.

5. See Testimony of Paul K. Krueger, U.S. Congress, House, Committee on Armed Services, Subcommittee on Seapower and Strategic and Critical Materials, *Hearings*, 98th Congress, 2d session, March 8, 1984, p. 289.

6. Fifty-eight commodities or commodity groups are included in the stockpile goals of the 1984 NDS program.

7. "The Input-Output Structure of the U.S. Economy, 1972," *Survey of Current Business* (February 1979), pp. 34–58.

8. The analysis above is based on Paul K. Krueger, FEMA, "Modeling Future Requirements for Metals and Minerals" (Paper presented at Pennsylvania State University, October 4, 1976).

9. Testimony of Paul K. Krueger, p. 289.

10. A description by an official of the Federal Preparedness Agency of the procedure for determining stockpiling goals identified three civilian tiers— essential, general, and phantom. The phantom tier consists mainly of luxury personal consumption items, the strategic material requirements for which would have no claim on the stockpile and no priority in the allocation of available materials. U.S. Congress, Senate, Committee on Banking, Housing, and Urban Affairs, *Hearings; Strategic Stockpile Policy*, 95th Congress, 2d session, November 14, 1978, pp. 87–90.

11. An internal FEMA memorandum made available to me used the thirty-fifth probability percentile as acceptable for the industrial base tier, the seventieth percentile for the essential civilian tier, and above the ninetieth percentile for the defense tier. These limits may not be currently in use, since the minimum probability percentiles presumably change from time to time.

12. Testimony of Paul K. Krueger, p. 289.

13. Ibid.

14. In March 1984 there was no stockpile goal for alumina, but there were goals for aluminum and certain grades of bauxite. FEMA, *Stockpile Report, October 1983–March 1984*, p. 22.

15. For a description of the AMP process, see ibid., pp. 11–12; and Testimony of Paul K. Krueger, pp. 285–87.

16. This interpretation is given in Department of Commerce, *Critical Materials Requirements of the U.S. Aerospace Industry* (Washington, D.C., 1981), pp. 222–23.

17. The last reported release of stockpile materials under the presidential peacetime authority occurred on November 5, 1979, when President Carter released 1,000 short tons of high-quality chrysotile asbestos to the Department of Defense. This was the first such release since the 1973 release of quinine and the twenty-eighth release in the history of the stockpile program. FEMA, *Stockpile Report, October 1979–March 1980*, p. 11.

4

Major Criticisms of the NDS Program

The NDS program has been subjected to a broad range of criticisms throughout its history, some of which have led to changes in the program. The criticisms by the Symington committee that stockpile objectives were adjusted to support domestic mining interests rather than national security and that there were excessive profits and irregularities in contracts for deliveries to the stockpile led to changes in the 1979 stockpiling act with respect to setting stockpile objectives and acquiring inventories. Other criticisms and recommendations by the Symington committee were not dealt with, however. Presidents Kennedy and Nixon criticized the size of the stockpile, and prominent legislators and specialists outside government have criticized the assumptions used in determining stockpile goals. This chapter seeks to evaluate the major criticisms of the current NDS program.

Unrealistic War Emergency Assumptions

A frequent criticism of the present NDS program is that the assumption of a three-year conventional war is unrealistic in a nuclear age. This criticism must be interpreted as a judgment that the assumed war scenario is less probable than some others, such as a strategic nuclear war in which a substantial portion of the U.S. economy would be severely damaged. Given the present balance of strategic nuclear capabilities between the United States and the Soviet Union, a conventional war in Europe with a simultaneous war in another region, such as an attack on Japan, cannot be regarded as highly improbable. It might be argued, however, that the present stockpile program assigns too high a probability to a three-year conventional war in relation to the probabilities of other emergencies and by doing so causes a misallocation of the resources available for national defense. If a strategic nuclear war and a long-term conventional war were both assigned the same probability, some of the expenditures now planned for the stockpile program might better be allocated to stock-piling finished goods rather than the strategic materials for producing them. Indeed, a similar point was made by the munitions board during the Eisenhower administration in arguing that taking fewer calculated risks in stockpiling than in other defense programs was unjustified (see chapter 2).

It is not possible to prepare for every conceivable contingency that might involve the defense of the nation, including the maintenance of civilian consumption during a war. Risk is unavoidable, but we can reduce risk by taking account of the probabilities of various contingencies. Most political analysts would probably agree that a disruption of imports of cobalt from Zaire or of chromium from South Africa and Zimbabwe (which account for over half the non-Communist world output of cobalt and chromium respectively) is more likely to occur than a three-year conventional war involving the United States and the Soviet Union. Yet these peacetime disruptions for the nondefense sector are not taken into account in the stockpile. Senator William Proxmire has criticized the stockpile goals for the nonessential civilian sector of the economy as much too large in relation to the probability of a three-year conventional war.[1]

Another aspect of the NDS war scenario that has been challenged is the assumption that the United States would have one year's advance warning of a three-year conventional war. According to the testimony of an official of the Federal Preparedness Agency (the predecessor of FEMA), the longer the warning period, the larger the stockpile that would be needed to expand military production before the expected conflict.[2] Although World Wars I and II began well before the United States became involved and in both preparation for war was limited, the assumption of a year's warning for a conventional war involving the Soviet Union has been seriously criticized by Senator Proxmire and others. In fact, Proxmire stated that the assumption contradicted Department of Defense contingency planning, which assumed little or no warning of war.[3]

Selecting a highly precise war scenario among many conceivable events as the foundation for calculating materials requirements and supplies might be more acceptable if it were a worst-case scenario that was highly likely to occur. No evidence has been provided, however, that the existing war scenario meets this criterion. A worst-case scenario should not be limited to a single contingency but should envision a series of events over ten or fifteen years, during which one or two regional wars and a conventional war might occur, followed by a stalemate in which much of the world's ocean shipping would be restricted for five years or more. The probability of the worst-case scenario may be too low, however, to warrant the enormous inventories of strategic materials required for the defense, essential civilian, and industrial base tiers. The allocation of defense expenditures for the NDS must also be related to an assessment of the probabilities of a wide range of other contingencies affecting national security. Reaching agreement on the most probable war or nonwar scenario that would disrupt imports would be exceedingly difficult, but we might be able to reach some agreement on the relative probability of each of a number of scenarios over a ten- or fifteen-year period.

Improper Methods of Determining Stockpile Goals

A number of criticisms have been made of the current methods of determining stockpile goals, given the war scenario assumed. The American Mining Congress (AMC) has for decades argued that stockpile goals should be calculated as a certain percentage or multiple of annual imports of each strategic material, and several bills embodying the AMC proposal have been introduced in Congress. The AMC argument as advanced by its spokesman, Simon D. Strauss, is that wartime and peacetime requirements of strategic materials have in the past been about the same, although they have been distributed differently between defense and nondefense uses.[4] Not only would the AMC method eliminate the need for elaborate projections of a wartime mobilization economy, but a simple rule based on imports would avoid changing stockpile objectives, which in the past have led to large disposals of excess inventories. Although the mining industry has supported the strategic stockpile, it has been highly critical of stockpile policies that give rise to uncertainty in markets for minerals.

An objection to the AMC proposal is that there is little rationale for creating a stockpile equal to a certain percentage of recent imports of each imported strategic material. The size of the stockpile of a material would not be related to the vulnerability of the import source to disruption, to the degree of U.S. dependence on imports of the material, or to the importance of the material to defense or civilian production. To take an extreme example, why should the United States establish a stockpile for iron ore equal to 100 percent of annual imports, when the United States is potentially self-sufficient in iron ore and two-thirds of its imports come from Canada? To be fair to the AMC position, it does recognize exceptions to the use of a standard import formula in such cases; but there are unique circumstances for each imported material, and applying a general formula for stockpiling to most of them would create a stockpile that would provide much less security than could be obtained at the same cost with a different composition of materials. As discussed in chapter 5, however, the import formula could be modified to meet this objection.

Criticisms have also been made of the inclusion of nondefense materials requirements in the stockpile, especially of nonessential civilian requirements. Before the Eisenhower administration, when stockpile objectives were mainly for materials needed for defense production, many congressmen argued strongly for the inclusion of materials needed for the production of civilian goods and services in wartime. If the stockpile program allows for the production of civilian goods, how much austerity is to be imposed on the civilian economy? Actually, the amount of austerity will depend on the nature of the war. Modeling a war mobilization program on World War II arbitrarily determines the degree of civilian austerity. It is unlikely that a war in the Middle East in which the United States is directly involved would call for the same degree of civilian austerity as that envisioned in the present assumption of a two-front conventional war.

Not only will each war emergency call for a different degree of civilian austerity, but there is no reason to believe that a future war mobilization must follow the World War II pattern of price controls, rationing, and government allocations. Some people believe that in periods of shortage the price system will do a better job than government controls of allocating resources to achieve national economic objectives. Moreover, a system of competitive prices accompanied by appropriate macroeconomic controls is more likely to promote adjustments to the shortages, including the use of substitutes and conservation, that would maximize the welfare of the civilian sector within the constraints determined by defense production.

Another criticism of stockpile goals is that they are not justified by the application of social benefit-cost accounting.[5] The size of the stockpile is socially optimal if the probability-adjusted social benefits derived from releasing the last unit of the stockpile are equal to the additional social cost of maintaining the last unit in the stockpile. Although the application of social benefit-cost analysis to the stockpile goals for the defense tier might be difficult and perhaps impractical, there are methods of determining the socially optimal stockpile for the civilian sector of the economy.[6]

Failure to Deal with Peacetime Import Disruptions

As noted in chapter 2, many government and nongovernment spokesmen have been concerned about the vulnerability of the U.S. economy to disruptions of imports of strategic materials in peacetime and the effects of such disruptions on both the defense program and the civilian economy. Indeed, much of the rationale given for the stockpile program has involved the high probability of import disruption in the form of cartels, embargoes, and limited wars for commodities such as bauxite, chromium, cobalt, and manganese, for which the United States depends almost entirely on foreign sources. Yet the present NDS program does not deal with this issue.

Although President Carter promised to address this problem, there is no record of his taking any action, nor is there any record of the problem's being considered by the Reagan administration. In his April 1982 *Report to the Congress on the National Materials and Minerals Program Plan,* President Reagan referred to peacetime "shortages or cutoffs" of minerals in connection with the implementation of Title I of the Defense Production Act, which authorizes various forms of assistance to domestic production. The section of the report dealing with the NDS program discusses stockpile acquisition and use only in connection with the three-year-war scenario. But for reasons discussed in chapter 5, promoting domestic production cannot be a substitute for stockpiling materials for which domestic commercial resources are very small or nonexistent.

The vulnerability of the civilian economy to disruption of imports of materials for which this country is highly dependent on foreign sources can be dealt with in three ways: the stockpiling act can be amended to permit releases of materials for civilian production, and NDS inventories can be increased to allow for such contingencies; the U.S. government can establish an economic stockpile designed for import disruptions in peacetime; or private inventories can be accumulated in amounts sufficient to compensate for possible disruptions. Congress and the administration appear to have little interest in the first two alternatives. Whether private inventories are sufficient to prevent serious damage to the civilian economy from the disruption of imports and whether they might be made sufficient by some form of government subsidization are discussed in chapter 5.

A possible answer to the criticism that the NDS program does not deal with the vulnerability of the economy to import disruptions of minerals in peacetime is that the probabilities of such contingencies and the potential losses to the economy are not large enough to justify the cost of stockpiling the commodities. This question has been dealt with by several private and governmental studies for a handful of minerals in the past, but much more empirical and theoretical work needs to be done.[7] The cost to the economy of a substantial cutoff of imports would arise from the increase in the price of the restricted commodity. Since the short-term elasticity of demand for most minerals is quite low, even a modest reduction in import supply is likely to cause a several-fold rise in price. Sources of most imported minerals are widely diversified, however, and a peacetime disruption is likely to take place in only one source at any one time. My tentative conclusion is that a stockpile for dealing with possible peacetime disruptions is likely to be cost effective for only a few minerals. The strongest case can be made for cobalt and chromium, with weaker cases for manganese and platinum-palladium.[8] There may be other materials for which government-sponsored stockpiling would be cost effective.

Discouragement of Private Inventories

Private stocks of strategic materials serve virtually the same function as government stockpiles during supply disruptions. It is argued that government stockpiles may discourage the accumulation of private inventories, so that the potential benefit of a government stockpile is offset by a reduction in private stocks. This argument assumes that in the absence of a government stockpile and of the expectation of government controls in periods of import disruption, private inventories will increase to the point at which the estimated probability-adjusted capital gains from holding the last unit of stocks accumulated are equal to the additional cost of maintaining the last unit of inventory (including interest and storage costs). The existence of a government stockpile that would be released in the event of an import disruption reduces the expected capital gains from accumulating private inventories and therefore reduces the accumulation of private stocks by the amount of the government stockpile. If it is assumed that the private sector has the same objectives as the government in accumulating stocks and that both have the same information on which to base the probability of an import disruption and the same degree of aversion to risk, private inventories would be equal to the optimum government stockpile. No private stockpile for dealing with potential import disruption would be accumulated if a government stockpile of the optimum size existed.

On the basis of this analysis, several economists have expressed serious doubts about the cost effectiveness of the NDS as contrasted with reliance on private inventories responsive to market incentives. For example, a 1979 study prepared under contract with the Federal Preparedness Agency concluded that "the potential effects of the existence of the strategic stockpile on private action will call into question the basic rationale for the establishment of the strategic stockpile."[9] There are difficulties, however, in applying this analysis to the NDS.

The effect of the NDS on private inventories depends on several objective conditions as well as on the behavior of private inventory speculators. One question is whether private entities actually hold inventories in anticipation of a major war. This seems unlikely with or without a government stockpile since it is well known that the government's mobilization plan for a major war calls for price controls and allocations of strategic materials. Under those conditions speculative holdings could not be legally sold for a profit large enough to justify the cost of holding, and even a manufacturing firm holding strategic materials for its own use might not be able to pass on to consumers the scarcity value of the materials. Speculators would undoubtedly hold inventories for peacetime disruptions of supply if they were convinced that the government would not impose price controls or special taxes on their capital gains and that materials from the NDS would not be released to counteract a peacetime shortage.

Suppose the government were to announce that private inventories of strategic materials would not be subject to direct or indirect price controls during a period of import disruption, whether in peacetime or in wartime, and that the government held no stockpile. Under these circumstances it is unlikely that private inventories would approximate stockpile goals that the government would regard as sufficient to meet requirements for defense and civilian production during a major war, for several reasons.[10] First, private firms would not have access to the same information as the government; even if they did, they would be unlikely to reach the same conclusions about the probability of a major war or the effects of such a war on supplies of strategic materials. Second, risk factors employed by the private sector in calculating costs and capital gains are unlikely to be the same as risk factors employed by the government. Third, private profit maximizers would not take into account externalities, in the form of the effects of increases in prices on the functioning of the economy as a whole, that would be taken into account by the government in establishing stockpile goals. Finally, private speculators could not take into account war mobilization plans that might be known only to the government.

Although it is highly unlikely that private inventories would approximate government stockpile goals in the absence of a government stockpile, would it be possible for the government to reduce its stockpile goals by encouraging private inventory accumulation? Or would every dollar spent for the government stockpile be offset by an equal decrease in private accumulation? The latter would be the case only if the government planned to release stockpile material during every import disruption for which private inventory accumulation was undertaken. If the government adopted a policy of stockpile releases only in the event of a major war, private inventory accumulation would take place in anticipation of import disruptions in peacetime. Since it would serve the same purpose as the government strategic stockpile in time of war, its encouragement through some form of subsidization would enable the government to hold a smaller strategic stockpile. Private inventory accumulation might be further encouraged if the government announced a policy of not imposing price controls on strategic materials in wartime. Moreover, some would argue that there are strong reasons for allowing free markets in materials during wartime.

Administrative Rigidity and Inefficiency

Even those who support the rationale and objectives of the present NDS program are well aware of serious shortcomings in its administration, many of which derive from the legislative framework. Before the 1979 stockpiling act was passed, extensive criticism was voiced in Congress of the use of the NDS program for purposes other than national defense. Therefore, the 1979 act greatly restricted the administrative flexibility through congressional oversight of changes in stockpile inventories. This oversight has limited the ability of administrators to change the composition of stockpile inventories in line with stockpile goals by selling excess inventories and using the proceeds to acquire materials whose inventories are short of the goals. Holding inventories valued at nearly $4 billion in excess of goals constitutes a needless cost. Although large excess inventories should not be dumped on the market in any one year, disposals have been unnecessarily slow. Congress has withheld authority to dispose of some 138 million ounces of silver, for which there has been no stockpile goal for a number of years, and the NDS missed an opportunity to sell when the price was substantially higher than it is now.

Even within the framework of existing stockpile legislation, the management of the NDS program has been regarded as severely deficient. The complex interagency structure, with more than a dozen cabinet-level departments and agencies involved in determining stockpile goals and the AMP for stockpile acquisition and disposal, is alleged to contribute to the inefficiency of the program. In November 1984 the National Strategic Materials and Minerals Program Advisory Committee recommended that the NDS program be administered by a government corporation. This recommendation was based on the finding that "efficient, sound, business-like management of the stockpile is difficult under the present system in which decision-making authority is so widely distributed among disparate agencies with corresponding disparate missions."[11] Dissatisfaction with the NDS was also the motive for the introduction of H.R. 33, which would transfer management of the NDS to the secretary of defense, a responsibility that the Department of Defense denied it wanted.[12]

A serious criticism of the NDS is that many materials in the stockpile—some of them purchased thirty years ago—have deteriorated so as to impair their usefulness or have become technologically obsolescent in the sense that their specifications no longer meet current industrial requirements. Some of the materials are not in the form required for modern industry, given the shortage of domestic facilities for processing ores into metals or alloys. A 1982 report by the National Materials Advisory Board states:

> It appears that past management of the stockpile has almost exclusively emphasized the quantitative aspects of the stockpile and has been excessively ad hoc in character. There is need for a regularization and formalization of stockpile decision making, especially as regards the *qualitative* attributes of stockpile materials (form and grade).[13]

A 1983 study by the American Society for Metals concluded that the pre-1980 cobalt stockpile "cannot be relied upon for the most critical usage."[14] Metallurgical processing to upgrade some older materials will be required. The longer-run solution is to rotate older materials frequently in the stockpile. The 1979 stockpiling act authorizes the upgrading of materials and their rotation, but these have not been done, because of either a lack of funds or administrative ineptitude.

From the beginning of the NDS program, Congress has authorized and encouraged the barter of surplus agricultural commodities for strategic materials; these materials have been added to the stockpile, often with little justification in terms of national security. Extensive barter programs were undertaken during the 1950s and 1960s, but thereafter barter was not employed until the exchange of surplus agricultural commodities for Jamaican bauxite in 1982 and 1983. Most economists have deplored the practice of circumventing the normal market process because it is inefficient and usually costly. Often the United States receives less material per bushel of wheat or pound of butter than it could obtain if it sold the agricultural commodity at the world market price and purchased the strategic material at the lowest competitive price. Moreover, since barter usually entails selling agricultural commodities below U.S. market prices, the transactions amount to an export subsidy in violation of rules of the General Agreement on Tariffs and Trade (GATT).[15]

Limited National Defense Orientation

The NDS is also criticized for its narrow concept of national defense. Considerable ambiguity attaches to the concept of national defense, but many view it broadly as maintaining an industrial and technological base capable of supporting a strong defense program for meeting threats to national security, not simply as the defense capability of the economy in time of war. The NDS was initially conceived as a stockpile of materials likely to be in short supply during a major war such as World War II, but determining stockpile goals by simulating World War III has been unsatisfactory to many policy makers concerned with national defense. Therefore, some fault the NDS program for failing to take account of contingencies leading to shortfalls of strategic materials required for both defense production and for maintaining the industrial base during peacetime.

As noted in chapter 2, the administration's argument that the NDS program should provide strategic materials for the industrial base tier in a period of war mobilization but not in peacetime is regarded as inconsistent with a broad concept of national defense. If supplies of chromium, cobalt, and manganese were substantially reduced because of a regional conflict in Africa, the industrial base might be impaired, with adverse consequences for the defense program. If, as some military specialists believe, no equipment will be used in the next war that has not been produced before the war, the availability of materials for the industrial tier may be more important for defense production in peacetime than during a war.

The argument against this criticism is that in peacetime a free enterprise economy with good government policies can achieve maximum growth and a strong industrial-technological base and can deal with contingencies such as import disruptions without special government protection. The national defense argument is frequently used by those wanting protection from import competition, government assistance in times of economic shocks, or tax benefits or subsidies for certain industries. Such government activities are more likely to weaken the national economy and defense. Only in periods of major war, when the government commandeers a very high portion of national resources and international trade is seriously restricted, should the government assume responsibility for an adequate supply of strategic materials as well as for many other aspects of national economic welfare.

There is much to be said for the latter position. The government is expected to provide assistance to the civilian economy in time of national emergency, however, whether in the form of earthquakes, floods, or widespread economic dislocation. The question then becomes whether a sudden cutoff of normal imports of strategic materials constitutes a national emergency to which the government should respond.

Notes

1. Proxmire advocated reducing the projected 1978 cost of acquiring stockpile goals by $6.3 billion (55 percent of the total) by eliminating the provision for the general civilian tier. He also stated, "We could eliminate the ridiculous assumption about prewar industrial mobilization and save $3 billion." U.S. Congress, Senate, Committee on Banking, Housing, and Urban Affairs, *Hearings, Strategic Stockpile Policy,* 95th Congress, 2d session, November 14, 1978, pp. 1–3, 108.

2. Ibid., p. 59.

3. Ibid., pp. 73–74.

4. Testimony of Simon D. Strauss, U.S. Congress, Senate, Committee on Armed Services, Subcommittee on Military Construction and Stockpile, *Hearings, General Stockpile Policy,* 95th Congress, 1st session, September 9, 1977, pp. 60–64.

5. An internal memorandum of the FEMA staff described a method for relating the social benefits of the NDS to the social costs of maintaining the stockpile, given the assumptions for the war scenario the stockpile is designed to serve.

6. A socially optimum stockpile for the civilian sector could be determined in much the same way as a socially optimum economic stockpile. See Raymond F. Mikesell, "Economic Stockpiles for Dealing with Vulnerability to Disruption of Foreign Supplies of Minerals," *Materials and Society,* vol. 9, no. 1 (1985), pp. 90–98.

7. For a review of the literature on this subject, see ibid., pp. 59–128.

8. Ibid., p. 106.

9. Steven P. Dresch, "Allocation of Final Demand Expenditures in a Wartime Economy and Development of Strategic Stockpile Objectives: Assessment and Reformulation" (New Haven, Conn.: Institute for Demographic and Economic Studies, September 20, 1979, processed), p. 11. A revised version of this study was released in 1984. See "U.S. Strategic Stockpile Policy: A Critical Assessment of Anticipatory Governmental Action" (Laxenburg, Austria: International Institute for Applied Systems Analysis, July 1984, processed).

10. This issue was addressed in a study on economic stockpiling that examined whether the optimum private inventories and the optimum inventories held by a government economic stockpile would be approximately the same. National Commission on Supplies and Shortages, *Studies on Economic*

Stockpiling: Public and Private Stockpiling (Washington, D.C., September 1976), chaps. 3, 4.

11. This recommendation was issued in mimeographed form by the advisory committee, together with a background statement dated November 15, 1984.

12. U.S. Congress, House, Committee on Armed Services, Subcommittee on Seapower and Critical Materials, *Hearings on H.R. 33, to Transfer Management of the National Defense Stockpile to the Secretary of Defense,* 98th Congress, 1st session, February 22, 1984.

13. National Materials Advisory Board, *Considerations in Choice of Form for Materials for the National Stockpile* (Washington, D.C.: National Academy Press, 1982), p. 144. See also Committee on Assessment of the Need for Quality Determination of Nonfuel Materials in the National Defense Stockpile, *Priorities for Detailed Quality Assessments of the National Defense Stockpile Nonfuel Materials* (Washington, D.C.: National Academy Press, 1984).

14. American Society for Metals, *Quality Assessment of National Defense Stockpile Cobalt Inventory* (final report prepared for the Federal Emergency Management Agency) (Washington, D.C., August 30, 1983); reprinted in U.S. Congress, Senate, Committee on Armed Services, Subcommittee on Preparedness, *Hearings, National Defense Stockpile,* 98th Congress, 1st session, October 19, 1984, pp. 12–59.

15. These criticisms of barter arrangements were made by Robert A. Cornell, deputy assistant secretary, U.S. Department of the Treasury. Although he did not oppose all barter transactions, he indicated that the administration would discourage an extensive use of barter. Ibid., pp. 74–76.

5
Proposals for Changes in the NDS Program and for Alternative Approaches

Proposals for changing the present NDS program range from sharply reducing or even eliminating it to expanding the functions of the stockpile to deal with disruptions of imports in peacetime. They include proposals for government support of domestic production of strategic materials as a partial substitute for stockpiling. I have already mentioned proposals for improving the administration of the stockpile, but the administrative structure has gone through a number of changes in the past without apparent improvement in efficiency. Perhaps the greatest barrier to efficiency lies in the legislative framework and the budgetary constraints imposed by both Congress and the administration. It is not possible to have a stockpile program with maximum flexibility for formulating and implementing long-term goals while at the same time subjecting its administration to tight controls.

Amending the Stockpile Act to Permit Releases for Civilian Production during Peacetime

In chapter 4 I mentioned proposals to amend the stockpile legislation to permit releases for both defense and civilian production in periods of import disruption during peacetime. Those proposals would in effect combine the present functions of the NDS with those of an economic stockpile. Several important changes would be required. First, stockpile goals would need to be increased to allow for peacetime import disruptions as well as for a three-year war. Second, the process by which strategic materials would be released in peacetime would need to be altered from that contemplated for a wartime mobilization period during which materials would be allocated and price controls imposed. Allocation and price controls would be neither ap-

propriate nor publicly acceptable in peacetime. Hence stockpile releases for civilian use should be sold in competitive markets in much
the same way as releases from the Strategic Petroleum Reserve are to
be sold if petroleum imports are cut off.

Third, Congress would undoubtedly seek to define as precisely
as possible the conditions under which the president might authorize
stockpile releases during peacetime, to prevent the use of the stockpile for price stabilization (during periods when there are no import
disruptions from abnormal causes), for reducing inflation, or for bal-
ancing the budget. It was the use of stockpile releases for purposes
other than national defense that led Congress to specify conditions
for releases in the 1979 stockpiling act. Permitting stockpile releases
to be used for civilian production during peacetime would appear to
require an unambiguous set of guidelines for such releases. The
guidelines might specify the sources of foreign supply disruption,
the percentage of total normal imports affected by the disruption, and
the actual or anticipated effect on prices of the disrupted materials.

A fourth necessary change would be to formulate goals for
peacetime civilian use that would make the cost of maintaining the
stockpile bear some relation to the potential benefits to the civilian
economy. Although Congress has been willing to fund the present
NDS program at least partially for use in a war mobilization economy
without any justification through social benefit-cost accounting, it
would be irresponsible fiscal policy not to require such justification
for a civilian-oriented program in peacetime. Given all these necessary changes in strategic stockpile legislation and implementation, a
preferable strategy might be to establish a separate economic stockpile with appropriate guidelines rather than to combine the two
stockpile functions into one program.

Creating an Economic Stockpile

Creation of an economic stockpile has had considerable support in
and outside Congress and has been the subject of a number of studies
sponsored by governmental commissions and agencies.[1] Economic
stockpiling has never been supported by any administration, however, and has been opposed by the mining industry, largely on the
grounds that it might be used as a means of stabilizing mineral prices
or that it might create uncertainty in the market for minerals. One
reason for the widespread opposition to an economic stockpile is the
tendency to confuse it with domestic and international price stabilization proposals. There is also a great deal of misunderstanding
about how it would operate.

According to economists, a true economic stockpile would operate by releasing stockpiled materials through competitive price sales on the market only in the event of a severe import disruption arising from foreign embargoes, civil disturbances in principal producing areas, regional wars, or cartel actions that might raise world prices by a multiple of their normal competitive levels. Thus there would be no allocations or price controls, no direct interference with the freedom of the market, and no restrictions on international trade in stockpiled materials. The benefits from releases of stockpile materials would arise from the avoidance or moderation of the rise in world price of the material.

Goals for an economic stockpile would be established on the principle of social benefit-cost accounting. The social benefits expected from stockpile releases would be adjusted by the estimated probability of an import disruption of the stockpile material over the planning period—say, ten or fifteen years. If a stockpile release to mitigate or avoid the effect of a 30 percent reduction in normal imports of a material would produce social benefits of $2 billion and the estimated probability of occurrence over a ten-year period was 25 percent, the probability-adjusted social benefit would be $500 million.[2]

The principal costs incurred in stockpiling are storage, maintaining the quality of materials by rotating inventories or upgrading, and the interest on capital investment in the inventory. Acquiring the inventory is regarded as a capital cost that would be recovered during the life of the stockpile. The inventory for each material is socially optimal when the additional cost of maintaining the last unit acquired is equal to the additional (probability-adjusted) social benefit from the release of that unit.

Subsidizing Private Inventory Accumulation

The larger the private inventories of strategic materials, the smaller the government stockpile that would be needed. Private inventories also have an advantage in that private holders and speculators will hold materials in the form most suitable for the current production of end products and the material will be constantly rotated so that it will not deteriorate or become technically obsolescent. As pointed out in chapter 4, however, private inventories may be well below the socially optimum level. It has therefore been suggested that additional accumulations be subsidized by the government.

If firms using materials vulnerable to supply disruption normally maintain inventories equal to six months' requirements, whether in raw or semiprocessed form, they might be awarded subsidies if they maintained a twelve- or fifteen-month supply. The subsidy would not need to equal the full cost of carrying the additional inventories since the firms would benefit from larger inventories in the event of a foreign supply disruption that caused a substantial rise in world price.

The government might make low-interest loans for inventory accumulation that would become due when inventories declined below the target amount. An objection might be raised that the government would be subsidizing private benefits in the event of a sharp rise in world price, but social benefits would also arise because higher inventory accumulation would reduce transfers abroad and other social losses in the event of an import disruption. If the firms accumulating larger inventories were expected to pay the cost of their maintenance as well as some interest on government loans, the government and private holders of the inventories would share in the cost of maintaining inventories that would provide both private and social benefits.

Basing the Defense Stockpile on Annual Imports of Strategic Materials

As noted in chapter 4, there has been considerable support for basing stockpile goals on recent imports of strategic materials. This procedure would have the important advantage of simplicity but would be hard to justify without recognizing differences in the importance of the materials to be stockpiled for the defense program and the contingencies for which the stockpile was acquired. It would be possible, however, to establish a base-case stockpile for each strategic material equal to, say, 50 percent of the average annual imports of the material for the past three years; the stockpile goal for each material could then be adjusted to reflect its relative importance in the defense program and for contingencies involving import disruptions continuing for more than six months that might affect the defense program. A modified application of this approach is presented in chapter 6.

Subsidizing Domestic Production of Strategic Materials

From the beginning of the NDS program many congressmen and administration officials have favored domestic production of strategic minerals, both as a source of materials for the stockpile in place of imports and as a substitute for stockpiling.[3] Several nonfuel minerals for which the United States depends largely or wholly on foreign sources can be produced from low-grade domestic ore bodies but at a cost considerably higher than the normal world price. These minerals include chromium, cobalt, manganese, and platinum-palladium. At current world market prices, however, no domestic production of the first three metals is likely to take place in the absence of substantial domestic subsidies, and in no case would domestic production supply more than a fraction of U.S. requirements. Moreover, unless new reserves of these minerals are discovered, the domestic resource base would be exhausted within a few years.[4]

Subsidizing domestic production either as a source of materials for the stockpile or as a substitute for stockpiling is likely to be less cost effective than stockpiling low-cost imported materials. It is argued that an additional ton of domestic production per month is equivalent to a stockpile of six tons to be released over a six-month period. Stockpile releases of a particular material are unlikely to occur more than once or twice in a decade, but, in the event of a foreign supply disruption, a stockpile release equal to a substantial part of normal annual domestic consumption might be required. The small volume of domestic production could not provide the large amount of material required over a short period while foreign supplies were disrupted.

It is also important to compare the additional cost per ton over the normal world price of a mineral produced domestically with the cost of maintaining a stockpile of that mineral that would provide an equivalent benefit in the event of a foreign supply disruption. Assume that the annual cost of maintaining a stockpile, including interest, is 15 percent of the cost of acquiring it. (The acquisition cost is a capital cost that would be recovered when the stockpile is released or the program terminated.) If the additional cost per ton of domestic output is more than 15 percent greater than the world price, holding the stockpile would be cheaper. In 1985 domestic production of cobalt would require a subsidy of more than twice the free market price.

There is a debate within Congress, within the Reagan administration, and among public interest groups on the desirability of providing incentives to produce domestic minerals that cannot be produced profitably in competition with imports. In 1982 and 1983 several bills were introduced in Congress to provide funding for government purchases of domestic materials under Title III of the Defense Production Act of 1950. Those testifying in favor of these bills included officials of the Department of Defense and representatives of the American Mining Congress.[5] Since the government would contract to purchase minerals at prices above those producers expect to obtain in the market, the program would constitute a subsidy to domestic production. Although supporters emphasize the contribution of domestic production of these minerals to national defense, the strong support of the mining interests—particularly of companies with mining claims on areas having deposits of such minerals—suggests that the program is also being promoted in the interest of the mining industry.[6]

Some administration officials have opposed subsidizing the domestic production of low-grade minerals. David Stockman, director of the Office of Management and Budget, opposed government purchases of domestic materials at subsidy prices on the grounds that the United States should rely on the market to improve the competitiveness of American industries and that our national security objectives should be met by purchases for the national strategic stockpile at world market prices.

In testimony before the Subcommittee on Economic Stabilization on the Defense Industrial Base Revitalization Bill (H.R. 5540), Robert Wilson, director of the Office of Strategic Resources, Department of Commerce, stated:

> The Administration opposes provisions of the Bill that raise authorizations for Title III to $1 billion a year for five years. We do not plan to make use of Title III authority to subsidize domestic industry. Instead, the Administration intends to rely on the market place to improve competitiveness of our industries and help reduce dependence on foreign sources of critical materials.[7]

Wilson further stated that "proposed programs under Title III would constitute a major intervention in the commodity markets and could represent a substantial drain on scarce budgetary resources, and may contribute to world-wide overcapacity."[8] John D. Morgan of the Bureau of Mines also testified against funding Title III to subsidize domestic production of critical materials. Nevertheless, the secretary of defense favored government subsidization of domestic production but proposed that the programs be funded from the defense budget.[9]

In a report issued June 3, 1982, the General Accounting Office (GAO) raised serious questions about the economic efficiency of acquiring cobalt for the stockpile from domestic sources at $25 to $30 per pound when it could be purchased at $15 per pound or less from Zaire.[10] The GAO report also suggested that "federal incentives to foster domestic mining of limited reserves [of cobalt] could result in the unwarranted depletion of domestic supplies that might better be saved for future use" and that "mining marginally economic reserves of cobalt may not only be obtained at great economic cost, but at great environmental cost as well."[11] Some of the low-grade reserves of chromium and cobalt are in or near wilderness areas or areas proposed for wilderness designation. Environmentalists argue that mining strategic minerals in or near such areas would damage environmental amenities and that national security objectives can be achieved at far lower social cost through alternative measures.

Proposals to promote domestic production by means of purchase contracts and loan guarantees are not limited to minerals for which the United States relies primarily on imports. In the past the Defense Production Administration financed the expansion of domestic capacity for aluminum, copper, lead, and zinc through purchase contracts and loan guarantees. Recently a FEMA offical suggested that in view of the loss of smelting capacity for copper, lead, and zinc, the government should consider taking action under the Defense Production Act to promote the maintenance of domestic capacities in these metals as a susbtitute for increasing stockpile inventories that are less than current goals.[12] A number of U.S. smelters have been shut down because of high labor and energy costs, unwillingness or inability to finance pollution abatement equipment, competition from imports, or some combination of these.

Whether the U.S. government should subsidize the metal industry in one way or another in the interests of national security raises several important questions of national policy. How far should we carry the principle that the United States should be self-sufficient in strategic materials? Why should this principle be applied to certain basic materials and not to others, such as bauxite, or to a range of manufactured products for which the United States depends heavily on imports? Is there a danger that national defense will be used as a surrogate for unemployment or trade deficits in justifying the promotion of national self-sufficiency? Would not a judicious stockpiling program prevent these deviations from a liberal international trade policy in promoting national security?

The United States is vulnerable to disruption of foreign supplies not only of minerals but of processed metals such as ferrochromium, ferromanganese, and alumina. These and other processed materials are increasingly produced in countries that mine the raw materials. Proposals have therefore been made to subsidize metal-processing industries for imported ores and concentrates. Again, rather than subsidize high-cost U.S. domestic processing capacity for these metals, it would be more economical and less damaging to international trade to stockpile the processed products.

Promoting Diversification of Foreign Supplies

Vulnerability to disruptions of foreign supply is reduced by diversifying foreign suppliers. Peacetime supply disruptions are unlikely to occur in more than one country or geographic region at a time. A civil disturbance in South Africa, for example, that reduced supplies of manganese or chromium would have much less effect on the United States and other industrial country importers of these metals if there were larger producing capacities for manganese in Australia and Brazil and for chromite in New Caledonia and the Philippines. Manganese reserves in Mexico could also be further developed for availability in a major war.

Under the authority of the Defense Production Act of 1950, the U.S. government has in the past promoted the development of foreign sources of materials in areas believed to be relatively secure from supply disruption. U.S. direct foreign investment in developing countries with resources of strategic materials could be encouraged by loans and investment guarantees from the Overseas Private Investment Corporation (OPIC) and loans from the Export-Import Bank. The U.S. International Development Cooperation Agency has a program for assessing deposits of strategic materials in developing countries and for bringing together potential private investors and officials of foreign countries. Acquiring strategic materials at world prices from selected foreign sources for the NDS could promote the diversification of foreign supply and would be much cheaper than subsidizing the development of low-grade deposits in the United States.

Promoting Research and Development for Substitution and Conservation

Given time and price incentives, substitutes can be found for almost any mineral for many if not all of its industrial uses. Alternative processes may greatly reduce requirements of the mineral without sacrificing performance. Finally, imports of strategic materials can be substantially reduced by means of recycling.[13]

The U.S. government can promote the development and implementation of technologies to reduce import vulnerability in several ways: making research grants; directly developing and testing new materials; and developing products made from more abundant materials in place of materials likely to be in short supply in periods of import disruption. A few years ago, for example, cobalt was regarded as almost irreplaceable in jet aircraft engines, but the sharp rise in cobalt prices in 1978 and 1979 after the invasion of Zaire led to research and development (R&D) programs to reduce cobalt use in jet aircraft. Three alternative alloys containing between 18 and 0 percent cobalt were developed, and the noncobalt alloys are reported to have operating properties superior to those of the cobalt alloy. A better version of the engine in F-15 and F-16 military aircraft has been designed using a nickel-aluminum-molybdenum alloy containing no cobalt.[14]

These important substitutions for cobalt might not have been developed by private industry in the absence of the sharp rise in prices. It may be desirable, therefore, for the government to undertake such R&D directly or to subsidize private R&D at a time when private industry has no price incentive to undertake the necessary expenditures. Social benefits derived from having alternative processes available for use in the event of a supply disruption may be sufficiently large to justify government subsidies.

An example of research carried on by the government to develop substitutes for an important imported mineral is that undertaken by the Bureau of Mines in cooperation with aluminum firms to develop processes for producing alumina from sources other than bauxite, including clay and shale, the domestic resources of which are abundant. It would greatly increase the security of U.S. alumina supplies if a commercially viable plant were established to produce alumina from nonbauxite sources. Since the attempts made during the 1970s to form a bauxite cartel failed, however, and Australia became the world's leading bauxite producer, the U.S. aluminum industry has shown little interest in shifting away from bauxite, despite this country's almost total dependence on imported bauxite. Nevertheless, the Bureau of Mines has continued research on the recovery of aluminum from nonbauxite sources.[15]

Taking Account of the Requirements of Our Allies

The responsibility of the United States for meeting the strategic materials requirements of NATO and other allies in time of global conflict has been discussed in congressional hearings on the NDS stockpile. To my knowledge, however, assisting other countries has not been taken into account in determining stockpile goals. This omission may in part reflect the assumptions about a global conventional war that the NDS is designed to serve. It may be noted, however, that during World War II the United States, in cooperation with the United Kingdom, assumed responsibility for acquiring and transporting both defense and nondefense materials required by nearly all areas of the world not occupied by the forces of Germany or Japan. There were, of course, few stockpiles, and materials had to be gathered from South America, Africa, and those parts of Asia free of enemy control.

It may be argued that if the United States is to assume responsibility for meeting its allies' requirements of strategic materials in another major war, the responsibility should be shared with all Western developed countries. Ideally, each country's stockpile program should be formulated in accordance with an international plan for meeting global requirements in a period of war emergency. An international plan for dealing with a world shortage of oil is provided by the International Energy Program Agreement of the Organization for Economic Cooperation and Development, according to which each member agrees to maintain an emergency oil reserve and to share a portion of its reserve with other members whose supplies may be more severely restricted. An international program for stockpiling and sharing strategic materials would, of course, be much more complex. Each country, for example, might maintain especially large stockpiles of the strategic materials it exports.

In his April 1982 report to Congress, President Reagan stated, "This Administration will initiate and conduct periodic and ad hoc consultation and coordination of the strategic and security policy aspects of nonfuel minerals and associated processing capabilities among industrial countries which are consumers of key materials."[16] Little has been made public about the implementation of this initiative.

Notes

1. See, for example, Michael W. Klass, James C. Burrows, and Steven D. Beggs, *International Minerals Cartels and Embargoes: Policy Implications for the United States* (a Charles River Associates report) (New York: Praeger, 1980); Office of Technology Assessment, *An Assessment of Alternative Economic Stockpiling Policies* (Washington, D.C., August 1976); and National Commission on Supplies and Shortages, *Studies on Economic Stockpiling: Public and Private Stockpiling for Future Shortages* (Washington, D.C., September 1976). For a review of governmental and nongovernmental literature on economic stockpiles, see Raymond F. Mikesell, "Economic Stockpiles for Dealing with Vulnerability to Disruption of Foreign Supplies of Minerals," *Materials and Society*, vol. 9, no. 1 (1985).

2. The probability coefficient for an import disruption of a material over a period of years is estimated by combining estimates of the probability of disruption from a number of foreign sources or kinds of contingencies. For a description of the method of calculating probability-adjusted social benefits of stockpile releases, see Mikesell, "Economic Stockpiles," pp. 90–97.

3. A 1982 report issued by FEMA argues the case for subsidization of domestic production of cobalt in combination with the present NDS program. It argues that domestic production would reduce the size of the NDS goal for cobalt and would therefore reduce annual government purchases for the

stockpile. See Office of Resources Preparedness, "Alternative U.S. Policies for Reducing the Effects of a Cobalt Supply Disruption—Net Economic Benefits and Budgetary Costs" (Washington, D.C.: FEMA, August 1982, processed).

4. A. Silverman, J. Schmit, P. Oueneau, and W. Peters, "Strategic and Critical Mineral Position of the United States with Respect to Chromium, Nickel, Cobalt, Manganese, and Platinum" (Washington, D.C.: Office of Technology Assessment, June 15, 1983, processed). Some domestic platinum may be produced without a government subsidy.

5. For arguments favoring government purchase of domestic materials, see U.S. Congress, Senate, Committee on Energy and Natural Resources, Subcommittee on Energy and Mineral Resources, *Hearings, President's Materials and Minerals Program and Report to Congress*, 97th Congress, 2d session, June 29, 1982; see also "AMC Supports DPA Funding," *American Mining Congress Journal*, April 27, 1983, p. 3.

6. For example, testimony in favor of the bill amending the Defense Production Act of 1950 was given by the president of Noranda Mining, which holds a claim on the Blackbird low-grade cobalt ore body in the Salmon National Forest in Idaho. Senate, Subcommittee on Energy, *Hearings, President's National Materials Program*, pp. 163–77.

7. H.R. 5540 was introduced in the 97th Congress, 2d session, but did not pass. It was reintroduced as H.R. 13 in the 98th Congress, 1st session, January 3, 1983, but again did not pass. Testimony on H.R. 5540 to amend the Defense Production Act of 1950, U.S. Congress, House, Committee on Banking, Finance, and Urban Affairs, Subcommittee on Economic Stabilization, *Hearings, Defense Industrial Base Revitalization Act*, 97th Congress, 2d session, March 23, 1982, p. 33. Title III in the testimony refers to the Defense Production Act of 1950.

8. Ibid.

9. Ibid., p. 57.

10. General Accounting Office, *Actions Needed to Promote a Stable Supply of Strategic and Critical Minerals and Materials* (report to Congress) (Washington, D.C., June 3, 1982), pp. 12–14.

11. Ibid., pp. 12–13.

12. See Testimony of Paul K. Krueger of FEMA in U.S. Congress, House, Committee on Banking, Finance, and Urban Affairs, Subcommittee on Economic Stabilization, *Briefing on the Defense Production Act of 1950*, 98th Congress, 1st session, March 2, 1983, p. 20.

13. See Office of Technology Assessment, *Strategic Materials: Technologies to Reduce U.S. Import Vulnerability* (Washington, D.C., 1985).

14. See U.S. Department of Commerce, "Critical Materials Requirements of the U.S. Aerospace Industry" (Washington, D.C., October 1981, processed), pp. 79–80.

15. See National Materials Advisory Board, *An Assessment of the Minerals and Materials Substitution Efforts of the Bureau of Mines* (Washington, D.C.: National Academy Press, 1983), pp. 15–16.

16. White House, *National Materials and Minerals Program Plan and Report to Congress* (Washington, D.C., April 5, 1982), p. 20.

6
Conclusions

The principal conclusion of this study is that the objectives of the National Defense Stockpile are too limited in view of the present international environment and the defense responsibilities of the United States. The NDS program was based on the experience of two world wars, but it should be altered to reflect the political and military environment of the 1980s. Before World War II the United States maintained an isolationist foreign policy; except for concern about external influence in Latin America, national defense was largely conceived as protecting U.S. soil from aggression by a major foreign power. After World War II the United States became committed by treaty to the defense of Western Europe and the Asia-Pacific region and came to regard a number of other regions, including the Middle East, as areas of vital interest, which it might defend by direct military action. National defense has thus become global and is not confined to the defense of national territory or of the North American continent. The United States has fought two regional wars, each involving hundreds of thousands of troops, and regional wars seem more likely in the future than a conventional global war.

The United States must be prepared at all times for a variety of minor and major nuclear or conventional wars and for a broad range of disruptions of imports of strategic materials and intermediate manufactured products required both for the defense industries and for the supporting industrial base. In this defense environment a strategic stockpile designed primarily to meet the requirements of a simulated war mobilization plan for a three-year conventional war with one year's warning does not constitute a rational allocation of resources for defense. A war emergency is likely to occur on short notice in any of a dozen areas of the world, and our defense capability may depend almost entirely on what has already been produced rather than on what can be produced during an emergency.

Given a realistic appraisal of the defense environment and of the range of import disruption contingencies for strategic materials, how should stockpile goals be determined, and what level of funding should be provided? First of all, it is important to consider budget outlays for the NDS within the context of a set of priorities for all defense outlays. All defense expenditures should be based on an evaluation of contingencies that pose a threat to national security. Since it is impossible to prepare adequately for every conceivable threat to security, the resources available for defense must be allocated on the basis of calculated risks or estimated probabilities. In a dynamic political and economic world environment, history is not the sole or even the most reliable basis for probability analysis. In allocating funds for defense, for example, between an additional $1 billion for the NDS and an equal outlay for MX missiles or Trident submarines, both the estimated defense benefits and the probability of contingencies calling for their employment should be taken into account.

Given the allocation of defense funds for the strategic stockpile, how should the goals for individual strategic materials—which serve as guidelines for annual acquisitions within the budget allocation—be determined? A rational approach would be to determine the goals in accordance with the probability of occurrence of contingencies that might disrupt imports of individual materials, with allowance for their relative importance in the defense program. Such contingencies include civil disturbances and regional wars in major producing areas, limited wars such as the Korean or Vietnam wars in which the United States would be directly involved, and major nuclear and conventional wars of varying intensity and duration. Even in the absence of a major war, a series of events, some occurring simultaneously, that disrupted strategic mineral imports could seriously impair both defense production and the industrial base producing goods and services for defense and civilian use. Since a stockpile large enough to deal with all possible contingencies or combinations of contingencies would undoubtedly exceed budget allocations for the stockpile, goals for individual materials should reflect the probability of occurrence of each contingency.

The stockpile goals can be determined in several ways. One suggested method is to establish a maximum goal for each strategic material—say, three years' annual imports of the material. The actual goal would be calculated by multiplying the maximum goal by the combined probability coefficient for the occurrence of a series of import disruption contingencies during a ten- or fifteen-year period, weighted by both the estimated degree of import disruption (percentage of normal imports) and the estimated duration of the disruption.[1] The combined probability coefficient could conceivably be 100 percent of the maximum goal, but in most cases it would be far less. All contingencies believed to have a significant probability of occurrence would be included in the combined probability coefficient. The coefficients for each contingency would be estimated by a group of military, political, and economic specialists employing the Delphic method. Each calculated stockpile goal would then be adjusted downward by the possibility of substituting for the material and the time required to accomplish substitution in production. Further adjustments could be made to reflect the essentiality of each material and its importance for the defense program.

If it were decided that the NDS would be drawn upon only for defense uses during a war emergency or the imminent threat of such an emergency, strategic material requirements and supplies for defense production might be determined for each emergency for which the Department of Defense has formulated a military plan, that is, a NATO war in Europe, a war in the Persian Gulf, or an attack on Japan. Allowance might also be made for strategic materials needed for the military programs of the NATO allies and Japan in the context of an international stockpiling and materials-sharing program. The total stockpile requirements for each material would be determined by combining the defense requirements for all war contingencies, with proper allowance for the duration of each emergency and for its probability of occurrence over the planning period. Since preparation for each war emergency must involve a calculated risk—the United States cannot afford to be fully prepared for every conceivable emergency—the risk for the availability of defense materials for any war contingency should be comparable with that for other military preparation for that contingency.

It might be objected that the estimated probability coefficients would simply be educated guesses. But surely this method is superior to basing stockpile goals on a single arbitrarily determined war scenario and mobilization plan. Moreover, within the context of the present assumption of a three-year global war, estimates of the probable availability of supplies from various sources are currently used to determine total supplies of individual materials. It would therefore make sense to estimate probabilities for each of a number of emergency contingencies rather than base the NDS program on one contingency.

A strong argument can be made for limiting the NDS to materials required for military purposes during a war emergency. Since a large portion of the present stockpile goals consists of materials for use in the civilian economy during a long conventional war, the cost effectiveness of the program is questionable in light of the low probability that such a war will occur. Whether NDS materials should be released for nondefense purposes in peacetime is also debatable. Careful analysis of the probability-adjusted social benefits may show that they exceed the social costs. Moreover, the civilian economy would benefit from a stockpile release solely for defense production since more of the limited supply of the material would be available for civilian production. In addition, stockpile accumulations are more likely to substitute for private inventories if releases are available for nondefense production in peacetime. Clearly more research is needed on this question.

Whether the government should establish an economic stockpile if the NDS is not available to meet requirements of the civilian economy in peacetime is also debatable. Most investigators conclude that an economic stockpile would be cost effective for only a handful of materials, perhaps no more than half a dozen. Government subsidization of private inventories of strategic materials above a minimum level (in relation to annual consumption by each user) has a number of advantages over a government-operated economic stockpile, but much more research is needed on this question as well.

I strongly believe in the need for an NDS. Although I prefer private, free enterprise solutions to problems wherever possible, I reject the notion that private inventories are sufficient to deal with major import disruptions or that defense stockpiles will simply replace an equivalent amount of inventories accumulated by the private sector. I am equally convinced that stockpiling is more cost effective and entails less government interference in the economy than subsidizing the development of low-grade domestic deposits of strategic materials. Domestic production of chromium, cobalt, manganese, and platinum could at best provide only a small percentage of national requirements, and our long-run security might be better served by leaving them in the ground as reserves than by producing them at a cost substantially higher than the cost of maintaining adequate stockpiles.

The current administrative and budgetary arrangements for acquiring stockpile materials and disposing of excess materials are inefficient and costly. The need for congressional approval of the disposal of excess inventories requires the government to hold billions of dollars worth of materials at considerable cost and no benefit. The administration should be given authority to dispose of these materials with proper regard for effects on market prices and to use the proceeds to acquire materials to meet stockpile goals. The net investment in stockpile inventories should be subjected to the normal budgetary process.

Finally, serious consideration should be given to releasing stockpile materials through competitive auction rather than allocating them solely to defense industries in peacetime or to defense and civilian industries in the event of a major war. I fully realize that this suggestion is in conflict with the concept that materials in the NDS should be made available only for defense use except during a major war. I seriously question, however, whether government allocation is superior under any circumstances to distribution through the free market. Many industries produce for defense and for civilian consumption, and the defense program is supported in one way or another by the entire industrial base. Allocations create immense bureaucratic problems, and a two-price system—one for materials released from the stockpile and another for other sources—could lead to large-scale misallocation of resources. Allowing market prices of strategic materials to rise for all uses would promote maximum adjustment through substitution and conservation. The idea that whenever there is a shortage of an important commodity the government should ration that commodity and control its price is an anachronism in an administration that believes strongly in a competitive price system. The costly experience with government petroleum allocation in the 1970s produced widespread disillusionment about government allocation. Fortunately the government has decided to use the auction method for withdrawals from the Strategic Petroleum Reserve, and the same method might be applied to releases from the strategic materials stockpile.

Note

1. Assume that the estimated probability of a one-year disruption of cobalt imports from Zaire and Zambia (which supply approximately 50 percent of U.S. cobalt imports) over a ten-year period is 30 percent and that the estimated probability of a two-year total disruption of cobalt imports over the same period is 5 percent. The combined duration-weighted probability coefficient for an import disruption of cobalt over the ten-year period would be 25 percent. If the maximum stockpile goal for cobalt is three years' annual imports, the probability-adjusted stockpile goal would be nine months' imports.

Addendum

The White House *Press Release* of July 8, 1985, containing President Reagan's proposal for drastically reducing the stockpile goals did not give the underlying rationale for this reduction. This rationale will be provided in a report to be issued sometime in the future. It is clear, however, that the proposed stockpile requirements reflect substantial changes in the guidelines for determining stockpile goals. For example, the *Press Release* states that "both Tiers of the stockpile provide over one-year's peacetime levels of imports for such materials as chromium, manganese, cobalt and tantalum." This suggests that stockpile requirements are in part at least related to annual imports. It may also reflect a reduction in the war planning period despite the statement that "the National Defense Stockpile will be sufficient to meet military, industrial and essential civilian needs for a three-year conventional global military conflict, as mandated by Congress in 1979."

The major portion of the proposed reduction in stockpile requirements arises from a reduction in the materials that would be available for the production of consumer goods. According to the *Press Release*, "The new stockpile, unlike the one proposed in 1979, does not reflect the stockpiling of materials to ensure non-essential consumer production in a protracted military conflict." I have been advised that the decision to reduce the stockpile requirements for consumption goods is based on the expectation that materials required for nonessential civilian consumption will be available from private domestic stocks and unrestricted foreign sources through the operation of open markets. If this information is correct, it would appear that the new mobilization plan contemplates a greater use of the price system during the period of war mobilization than exists under the present plan.

Selected AEI Publications

Essays in Contemporary Economic Problems, 1986: The Impact of the Reagan Program, Phillip Cagan, ed. (1986, 362 pp., paper $10.95, cloth $20.95)

The Politics of Industrial Policy, Claude E. Barfield and William A. Schambra, eds. (1986, 344 pp., paper $9.95, cloth $20.95)

Protectionism: Trade Policy in Democratic Societies, Jan Tumlir (1985, 72 pp., $5.95)

Crisis in the Budget Process: Exercising Political Choice, Allen Schick, with papers by David Stockman, Rudolph Penner, Trent Lott, Leon Panetta, and Norman Ornstein (1986, 88 pp., $4.95)

The AEI Economist, Herbert Stein, ed., published monthly (one year, $24; single copy, $2.50)

AEI Foreign Policy and Defense Review, Evron M. Kirkpatrick, Robert J. Pranger, and Harold H. Saunders, eds. (four issues, $18; single copy, $5)

• *Mail orders for publications to:* AMERICAN ENTERPRISE INSTITUTE, 1150 Seventeenth Street, N.W., Washington, D.C. 20036 • *For postage and handling, add 10 percent of total; minimum charge $2, maximum $10 (no charge on prepaid orders)* • *For information on orders, or to expedite service, call toll free 800-424-2873 (in Washington, D.C., 202-862-5869)* • *Prices subject to change without notice* • *Payable in U.S. currency through U.S. banks only*

AEI Associates Program

The American Enterprise Institute invites your participation in the competition of ideas through its AEI Associates Program. This program has two objectives: (1) to extend public familiarity with contemporary issues; and (2) to increase research on these issues and disseminate the results to policy makers, the academic community, journalists, and others who help shape public policies. The areas studied by AEI include Economic Policy, Education Policy, Energy Policy, Fiscal Policy, Government Regulation, Health Policy, International Programs, Legal Policy, National Defense Studies, Political and Social Processes, and Religion, Philosophy, and Public Policy. For the $49 annual fee, Associates receive
- a subscription to *Memorandum*, the newsletter on all AEI activities
- the AEI publications catalog and all supplements
- a 30 percent discount on all AEI books
- a 40 percent discount for certain seminars on key issues
- subscriptions to any two of the following publications: *Public Opinion*, a bimonthly magazine exploring trends and implications of public opinion on social and public policy questions; *Regulation*, a bimonthly journal examining all aspects of government regulation of society; and *AEI Economist*, a monthly newsletter analyzing current economic issues and evaluating future trends (or for all three publications, send an additional $12).

Call 202/862-7170 or write: AMERICAN ENTERPRISE INSTITUTE
1150 Seventeenth Street, N.W., Suite 301, Washington, D.C. 20036